How important is performance driven CRM?
Here's what Gartner, Inc. has to say...

"Over the next five years, customer service-oriented performance metrics will emerge as key success factors in creating a more loyal, and profitable, customer base. Metrics will evolve from efficiency metrics (churn rates, call handling times, call scores, Web hits) to those that focus on effectively understanding, delivering to and managing customer expectations, both latent and explicit. The new metrics will include retention of profitable customers, identification of cross sell/upsell, uncovering of new service revenue opportunities, and delivery of service based on customer value.

"The challenge for the enterprise will be in establishing holistic metrics through an iterative process, in partnership with the internal and external customer. Success will go to those best able to set, fulfill, and manage customer expectations through a series of discrete, measurable activities that result in specific outcomes. Management will need to innovate as it moves from rhetoric about the customer to action on how to retain customers."

— *Michael Maoz,*
   Vice President and Research Director, CRM Strategies
   Gartner, Inc.

Performance Driven CRM

Performance Driven CRM

How to Make Your
Customer Relationship Management Vision
a Reality

STANLEY A. BROWN
and
MOOSHA GULYCZ

wiley.com

John Wiley & Sons Canada Ltd
22 Worcester Road
Etobicoke, Ontario
M9W 1L1

The National Library of Canada has catalogued this publication as follows:

Brown, Stanley A., 1946-
    Performance driven CRM : how to make your customer relationship management vision a reality

ISBN 0-470-83161-8

    1. Customer relations—Management. I. Gulycz, Moosha II. Title.

HF5415.5.B763 2002   658.8'12   C2002-900471-3

Production Credits
Cover & interior text design: Interrobang Graphic Design Inc.
Printer: Tri-Graphic Printing Ltd.

Printed in Canada
10 9 8 7 6 5 4 3 2 1

This book is dedicated to those that dare,
to those that choose to do the uncommon rather
than the conventional, to those that want to share,
and to those that believe in continuous improvement.

To Francesca Guava, for her exceptional, tenacious
and logical view towards life and people. If only we could
be like her all the time and experience all of her pleasant dreams.
—M.G.

And to the little people (HDW and ERW) . . .
our future is in your hands.
Be bold, daring and enjoy life to its fullest.
—S.A.B.

C O N T E N T S

What Is Performance Driven CRM?

There is no shortage of books, articles and seminars that describe and define what Customer Relationship Management (CRM) is and is not. Gartner Group, a reputed research organization defines CRM as follows:

> *[It] is a business strategy the outcomes of which optimize profitability, revenue and customer satisfaction by organizing around customer segments, fostering customer-satisfying behaviors and implementing customer-centric processes. CRM technologies should enable greater customer insight, increased customer access, more effective customer interactions, and integration throughout all customer channels and back-office enterprise functions.*

Definitions aside, while an organization may have the desire to improve its customer-centric focus and outcomes, CRM doesn't just happen. It needs an appropriate CRM vision, strategy, action plan and implementation. However, success may still be fleeting. To ensure that a mechanism (some may call it the strategy) to measure, monitor and manage performance driven CRM is required. And that is what performance driven CRM is all about.

Performance driven CRM is an ongoing mechanism, based on continuous improvement, whereby organizations can sustain lasting relationships and the ability to understand, anticipate, manage and personalize the experience with the organization's current and potential customers and employees. It starts with a clear understanding of:

a) customers and their needs

b) the organization and its competencies

c) the organization's commitment to quality service for both the internal and external customer.

It requires measures/standards and benchmarks and a mechanism to create change—change in process, actions, organizational structure and people competencies. CRM can survive only with continuous performance improvement. And that is what this book is about—the mechanism/route map on how organizations can do the following:

- Ensure that their CRM vision is kept relevant and alive by using performance information to cycle back to the vision each year for validation or change to reflect new customer needs.

- Maintain a focus on key areas required to achieve the overall CRM vision by analyzing the performance information and identifying if they are getting closer to the vision.

- Create the information required to align the organization against it's CRM vision. The information can show where staff changes are required.

- Build internal organizational commitment by showing staff the improvements that were made.

- Build and sustain customer loyalty by contributing information that assists in managing customer, business and internal organizational relationships.

- Identify requirements for change levers such as change management workshops, customer service training and new technology solutions.

    This book is not about the theory of CRM nor about the technology behind it. It is a practical, hands-on aid to assist an organization in being successful in achieving enterprise-wide CRM. But it is not about achieving but rather maintaining CRM. It takes up from where the book *Customer Relationship Management: A Strategic Imperative in the World of eBusiness* left off. It is based on actual practice, leading technology and proprietary research. It considers not only where organizations are today, but where they should be going.

The book that follows provides a framework that ensures that the CRM *vision* becomes reality and fosters a cycle of continuous improvement.

PART ONE: DETERMINING AND ALIGNING THE CRM VISION

The first part of the book includes a review of CRM and the importance of the CRM vision as a starting point in the achievement of performance driven CRM. It talks about what it is, the challenges and pitfalls and deals with some of the essentials in the creation of the CRM vision. It confirms why organizations must start with a desired end state, a CRM vision, and the alignment that must be considered prior to the establishment of the performance programs that will ensure lasting CRM.

While the need for CRM should be unquestioned, there still continues to be resistance to buy in. Why? Most probably because that vision, as with any vision, has to then be aligned within the organization.

> *Alignment means ensuring that in order to realize the vision, a strategy exists. All components of the CRM strategy must, of course, be focused in the same direction and work together to achieve the CRM vision. All components/divisions of the organization must also move in the same direction. This direction has to be clear enough so that without doubt, all individuals know where they are going and how they fit in.*

The CRM vision sets the stage. It describes the purpose, the route map, that shows where the CRM road will eventually lead and points the organization in that direction.

PART TWO: CREATING PD CRM— THE THREE PERFORMANCE PROGRAMS

Part Two of this book discusses the first step in achieving performance driven CRM—the translation of the CRM vision to a CRM strategy that encompasses customer needs, organizational competencies and a commitment to quality service. That is essentially the framework of performance driven CRM (PD CRM). We describe the three critical performance programs necessary to ensure enterprise-wide CRM. The second program, the Organizational Performance Program, ensures an ongoing understanding of the organization. The first, the Customer Performance Program, ensures an ongoing understanding of the customer. The final, third program, the Quality Service Performance Program, ensures an ongoing commitment to continuous improvement in quality service.

Essentially, the three performance programs are a framework that is built on performance measurement and performance management. Performance measurement captures and collects performance data, while performance management takes this data and uses it to make required and substantial changes to your business in the areas of your customer, your organization and your level of quality service. Fundamentally, these changes drive successful and lasting CRM change.

PART THREE: THE TOOLS TO BUILD AND ENABLE THE PERFORMANCE PROGRAMS

This part deals with the tools, templates and exercises to let you act on PD CRM immediately. These tools, methodologies and technologies build upon leading practices across a wide variety of industries and provide you with the capability to measure and gain an understanding of the customer, the organization and internal commitment. These tools will allow you to drive the performance programs and achieve increased knowledge of the customer, their habits and trends. It will allow you to fully implement the performance programs that will ensure that the organization is committed to continuous improvement. It includes the following:

- a continuous improvement framework built around a comprehensive *quality scorecard* that sets expectations, measures and provides the basis for coaching and training

- a positive and proactive method for providing employee feedback on performance—a *coaching program* that encourages staff performance improvement and aligns staff behaviors and responsibilities with your CRM vision

- an *employee performance agreement* process/template that supports effective communication of accountabilities, requirements and achievement between the employee and organization

- a self-assessment that captures how well your Quality Service Performance Program is doing and whether you are maximizing the benefits of your program

PART FOUR: LEADING PRACTICES IN CREATING PERFORMANCE DRIVEN CRM

What are required next are targets (where you want to get to in the short term) and stretch targets (where you hope to get to over a longer period of time) and the need for best practices to point you in the right direction and learn from the experiences of others. Many examples are provided in this part of the book. For one organization, this performance program included; a balanced performance scorecard, a corresponding customer service survey and a proactive customer issue management process. The scorecard encompassed all areas of measurement that were relevant to quality service. It was determined that not all areas of measurement held equal value in the quality equation. Therefore, each of the measurement areas within the scorecard was weighted according to priority and importance, meaning that some areas counted more than others.

The corresponding customer service survey supported and enhanced the performance data obtained through the scorecard. When developing the customer service survey, care was taken to ensure that the information obtained through the survey would be compatible and comparable to the scorecard information.

Finally, a proactive customer issue management process was developed. It took all customer issues, categorized them into relevant information groupings, and ensured enough detail to make the information useful without overloading the system with insignificant details. There was a balance between too much and too little information.

WHAT MAKES THIS BOOK DIFFERENT

Over the years, we have been part of various incarnations of programs designed to enhance customer satisfaction and revenue enhancement. Whether it be TQM, BPR or any other management acronym, there has always been a missing component, one which organizations have ignored either deliberately or perhaps subliminally. Performance does not improve without embedding performance measurement and management into the culture of the organization and without making it an essential part of the required continuous improvement. And it must be a balanced effort—a balance between the customer, the organization and the organization's commitment to quality service.

This book provides guidance on how to accomplish these things. Specifically, it provides:

- a proven best practice approach to achieve CRM, together with work steps, checklists, quizzes and planning templates

- case studies from organizations that have implemented various stages of CRM (including Fedex, USAA, Marriot, Nortel, Dupont, Honeywell, Capital One, Radio Shack, Sears)

- case studies from those organizations that have implemented or exhibited best practices in the key principles and technology of CRM

- white papers, proprietary research and best practices

If you are well along the route, you may pick and chose the chapters that have most meaning to you. If you are at the start of the process, follow Parts Two and Three to the letter and learn from the practices and pitfalls of others, as found in Part Four. If you still need convincing to start on this journey, begin at Part One and read through this step by step. Regardless of your starting point, enjoy the journey, as there will be many rewards at the end.

Part One

Determining and Aligning the CRM Vision: Overview

The CRM vision is the starting point in the achievement of performance driven CRM. It directs us to the desired end state and sets the course to start us on our journey. Without this vision, the road to successful CRM will be difficult, and without tailoring it to your current needs—your strengths and competencies, the speed to market required, and business benefits needed to substantiate the investment in the CRM initiative—only limited, and possibly only short-term success will be achieved. Chapter 1 provides you with the tools to revisit your vision to ensure that it will meet your future needs.

Those organizations with successful CRM initiatives have been effective in:

- keeping their CRM vision relevant and alive
- excelling in using performance information to cycle back to the vision each year for validation or change that reflects new customer needs
- maintaining a focus on key areas required to achieve the overall CRM vision
- analyzing the performance information to demonstrate that they are getting closer to the vision
- creating the information required to align the organization against its CRM vision

Chapter 2 addresses these subjects in an effort to ensure that you stay on the proven path and avoid the potholes and detours that so many have traveled. But first, are you ready to start?

CHECKLIST: ARE YOU READY TO START?

Here's an exercise to start you on your way. Answer the following questions about your readiness to create a CRM vision. A scoring guide and evaluation of your readiness to proceed can be found at the end of the checklist.

	To a very limited extent			To a very great extent
1. Customer segments are well defined.	1 2 3 4 5			
2. The company uses customer satisfaction surveys for understanding customer needs and what satisfies and dissatisfies customers.	1 2 3 4 5			
3. Human resources management practices empower all employees to participate in improvement initiatives.	1 2 3 4 5			
4. Employees at all levels receive the education and training they need to participate effectively.	1 2 3 4 5			
5. Senior executives are personally and visibly involved in demonstrating that improved customer satisfaction is a high priority strategic goal.	1 2 3 4 5			
6. Customer service performance measures exist at the organizational, departmental and individual job levels and are widely publicized and acted upon.	1 2 3 4 5			
7. Communication is frequent and informative.	1 2 3 4 5			

8. All employees are aware of their internal   1   2   3   4   5
   customers and suppliers.

9. The working environment is conducive   1   2   3   4   5
   to the well-being and morale of all
   employees.

10. The organizational hierarchy does not   1   2   3   4   5
    inhibit effective and constructive two-way
    communication over process improvement
    issues.

11. The company's values are clearly articulated 1   2   3   4   5
    and understood by all employees. They are
    constantly and consistently reinforced by
    the actions of all managers.

12. Goals for customer satisfaction make us   1   2   3   4   5
    stretch but are attainable.

13. The company encourages close   1   2   3   4   5
    collaboration and teamwork.

14. The employee performance appraisal,   1   2   3   4   5
    recognition and reward processes strongly
    promote involvement in delivering
    customer satisfaction.

15. Business processes are regularly reviewed   1   2   3   4   5
    to eliminate nonvalue-adding activities and
    improve customer satisfaction.

16. Relationships with customers are managed   1   2   3   4   5
    effectively and involve obtaining information
    from them to improve products and services.

17. Business cases for change are clearly   1   2   3   4   5
    articulated and validated.

18. Customer complaints are welcomed and resolved quickly and positively.
     1   2   3   4   5

19. Effective processes for determining current and future customer requirements and expectations are applied both systematically and rigorously.
     1   2   3   4   5

20. The strategic and business planning processes have a strong focus on customer service and produce clear objectives for improvement.
     1   2   3   4   5

Scoring:

Add up your scores on all 20 questions. If your score was:

- less than 40: This book will provide you with a strong foundation as you start to build an organization dedicated to performance driven CRM. Chapter 1 is a mandatory starting point.

- 40 to 74: You are only halfway there. A deeper understanding of your organization and its competencies is necessary. The performance programs described in Part Two are key to your achievement of performance driven CRM.

- greater than 75: You are well on the road. The book offers best practices of others to learn from as well as other advanced techniques. Pick and choose those chapters that give you the most relevant guideposts.

So how did you do? Are you ready to start on your journey?

Getting Started:

THE NEED FOR A CRM VISION TO DRIVE THE PROCESS

W here does one start? With performance driven CRM (PD CRM), you seem to start backwards because you begin with the desired end-state—the CRM Vision.

Let's go back to what differentiates performance driven CRM from CRM in its purest sense. While CRM is a business strategy that seeks to optimize profitability, revenue and customer access, performance driven CRM is more. It is an ongoing mechanism, based on continuous improvement, that allows organizations to sustain lasting relationships and gives them the ability to understand, anticipate, manage and personalize the experience with their current and potential customers and employees.

It starts with a clear understanding of :

- customers and their needs
- the organization and its competencies
- the organization's commitment to quality service—from both an internal and external customer perspective

It requires measures/standards and benchmarks and a mechanism to create change—change in process, actions, organizational structure and people competencies. CRM can survive only with continuous performance improvement.

There is no doubt that in today's business environment, it is becoming increasingly difficult to manage customer relationships profitably:

- Increasingly informed customers have more choice and are less loyal to their suppliers.

- New distribution channels and communication media mean that the customer interaction mix is more complex, difficult to integrate and potentially expensive.

- Delivery channels are increasingly complex.

- Numerous powerful technology enablers are now available but are expensive to implement, and historic returns are uncertain at best.

- Marketplaces and exchanges threaten to bring manufacturers closer to their customers—disintermediation.

These issues are widely recognized and, in response, most major organizations have initiatives under way ranging from sales force automation to web-enabled customer contact centers. These traditional CRM initiatives may be useful but they are definitely not performance driven CRM.

The initiatives described above are often tactical (like trying to make incremental changes quickly) rather than strategic or long term in nature. They are often responses to short-term customer or cost pressure rather than to long-term market drivers. For many organizations, it has proven difficult, if not impossible, to manage mutually beneficial relationships when:

- They are not able to measure the value of their customers.

- They lack insight into what their customers really need rather than what they think that they need.

- They have no strategic approach to how to treat different customers different ways.

The net result is that most organizations fail to target their limited resources at their most valuable customers. They fail to achieve a balance between customer value, the quality of the customer experience and the cost of delivering it. While there may be isolated examples of sales force automation or perhaps some enhanced desktop technology, there is a real risk that the individual initiatives do not fit with each other or with the organization's wider business strategy. The result is wasted investment, duplicated effort, incompatible business solutions and an increasingly inconsistent customer experience.

There is therefore a compelling need for a CRM vision that addresses many of the issues with which organizations typically struggle:

- Which customers should you target?

- How can you deal with rapidly increasing channel fragmentation and media complexity to communicate with your customers?

- How should you balance quality of experience, cost to serve and profitability of the customer?

- What is the appropriate level of CRM integration for your business?

- What is customer "insight," and how do you get and use it?

- What should you do with unprofitable customers?

DEFINITION

Let's start with a definition. The vision can be structured in many ways. In fact, there are probably several hundred books on this subject alone. The following is a quick summary on vision—what it is, why you need one, and how to develop it.

The vision should include some basic components:

- a vision statement about the future of the business (you may have a five-year vision, but you will also want a subcomponent that directs the organization to what it can accomplish within a realistic time frame, say 18 months)

- a mission statement explaining how the organization expects to do business

- a core values statement (or sometimes called guiding principles) explaining what is essential to the accomplishment of the mission and the fulfillment of the vision

- a description of standards against which it dares to be measured (sometimes this takes the form of a Customer Bill of Rights, which we will talk about in more detail later. You can look for it in Chapter 5.)

More than any other document, this vision statement is a reference point for those within the organization (the internal customers) as well as those outside (your external customers) and is something around which the whole organization can rally. Without a strong commitment to it, starting at the top, the organization will wander without purpose. Departmental silos will appear, isolating areas from one another, corporate investment may be misdirected and employees will become unfocused. And if this happens, the result might be staff turnover and suboptimal customer service and acceptable revenue and earnings growth. These are outlined in the chart below, but notice the focus on the customer (both internal and external) and the need for focus and direction.

Component	Key Questions
Business Vision	What is our overriding goal and desired future state?
	What is our commitment to survival, growth, profitability?
	Why are we in business, and what business are we in?
	Should we be in a single operating business or a diversified enterprise?
	If we opt for diversification, should our lines of business be related or not?
Target Customers and Markets	What markets do we want to target?
	Who should our customers be, and which of their needs should we try to satisfy?
Geographic Coverage	What geographic area should we serve?
	Should we compete regionally, nationally, multinationally or globally?
Principal Products and Services	What range of products and services will we offer?
Core Technologies	What kinds of technologies do we want to be involved in?

Basis of Competitive Advantage	What distinctive competencies will we maintain relative to competitors?
	What values will customers obtain from buying our products and services?
Values	What key corporate values and shared beliefs do we hold dear?

Here's one variation of this series of statements for a division of DuPont, its Global Services Business (GSB).

CASE STUDY
DuPont Global Services Business

DuPont is an industrial company with three main business segments: fibers and intermediates, specialty chemicals and materials and specialty plastics and films. The internal Global Services Business (GSB) was created to provide support to all strategic business units (SBU) and employs about 6,000 staff. The GSB provides over 50 service offerings, and each of these contains multiple subofferings.

According to Jim A. Sinex III, manager, Customer Care Services, DuPont Global Services Business, the challenge for Dupont was to create a vision and rallying point for its divisions given a desire to operate GSB like a service business, providing clients with integrated solutions from a customized array of fully competitive, demand-driven offerings priced at full operational cost plus renewal.

To support its business strategy and put its vision into action, it was necessary for the business unit to incorporate DuPont core values in all GSB activities and develop and sustain a preferred business partner relationship with clients. This was to ensure that GSB could evolve toward a service company culture (i.e., knowledge, human capital based). It was also necessary to continuously renew employee capabilities/key competencies and GSB physical assets/IT infra-structure to sustain/improve the value added of its offerings and make the GSB an attractive place to work.

The challenge was that GSB had to operate as a demand-driven business, with a broad portfolio of offerings priced at full opera-tional cost plus renewal. It was also necessary to continuously renew offerings to provide ever-increasing value to its clients based upon its increased understanding of their strategies and knowledge of the external environment. This led GSB to create and implement a robust company-wide performance improvement process, which allowed it to selectively seek profitable external business at market price. It also aggressively pursued integration, standardization, reengineering and other productivity improvement opportunities in all geographic regions within the GSB.

Using the framework described above, the following is the artic-ulation of the GSB's CRM vision.

Component	Key Answers
Business Vision	We will be recognized and sought out as a premier integrated services business and *the* preferred partner to DuPont businesses. In doing that, we will help DuPont businesses do business better.
Target Customers and Markets	All strategic business units (SBU) of DuPont, globally.
Geographic Coverage	Global business units of DuPont
Principal Products and Services	The internal Global Services Business (GSB) was created to provide support to all strategic business units (SBU). The GSB provides over 50 service offerings, and each offering contains multiple subofferings.

Core Technologies	n/a
Basis of Competitive Advantage	The GSB will position itself for long-term viability by defining and implementing opportunities to improve the variability of offerings and by addressing "for profit," for "growth" and "third-party competition." That is, it will ensure that it is more competitively priced and adds more value (than competitive third-party offerings). We will price offerings to clients to cover all costs, including sufficient funds to ensure renewal of offerings and supporting capabilities and competencies and price offerings to external customers at "market." In addition, GSB will make all decisions (e.g., offerings design and delivery, resource allocations) to maximize value creation for DuPont and its businesses globally (versus any specific region or offerings group) and build on strength of existing client relationships by forming effective, enduring client partnerships based upon mutual dependency and shared responsibility for results.
Values	• Foster a culture that recognizes and rewards entrepreneurship, teamwork, risk-taking, holistic and integrated thinking, business results and client satisfaction. • Provide meaningful opportunities for GSB employees to have a fulfilling career in a successful DuPont business. • Deliver all services on a demand-driven basis and always deliver what we promise.

- Continuously renew our offerings in anticipation of or response to client needs.
- Be fully competitive with external service options based upon overall value, and take appropriate actions to address any offerings that aren't competitive.
- Migrate to common global offerings where appropriate while preserving local offerings for unique needs.
- Leverage offerings across businesses when supported by a strong business case (e.g., Order-to-Cash, Requisition-to-Pay, Process Design to Plant Operation).
- Systematically improve the business value added of all aspects of the GSB (e.g., offerings, work processes, IT systems) based upon objective external benchmarking, application of best practices and a clear understanding of client needs.
- Utilize both client and employee feedback as a major factor in guiding our behavior and offerings design and delivery.
- Manage our performance against key metrics and objectives using disciplined business processes.

DuPont was able not only to articulate, but also live these values to the benefit of its customer base—true CRM. How does an organization like DuPont do this, and what steps must be followed. Read on.

CREATING THE VISION

First, a CRM vision cannot be created as a bottom-up initiative. It must be produced and fine-tuned by senior management and must be revisited, at a minimum, on a yearly basis. It must be compatible with your current and/or future customer base and for that reason, customer-needs research or environmental scanning must be done before you begin to prepare this statement. As it drives the alignment of resources of the organization (human, financial and physical), the heads of these divisions must be involved in the process.

Some find it helpful to begin with a template, or a copy of another organization's statement, to start the process and then pick and choose what they like. Others commence with a clean sheet of paper and do not wish to be influenced by what others have done. Both methods work well, as long as the ultimate objective is to produce a simple statement that is realistic and written in clear everyday language. It must be realistic and believable or it will not be followed.

Hammer out this statement and then polish it. It will probably take a few iterations before it is just right. Only then will it be ready to be communicated. This will not be an easy process. Organizations generally invest quite a bit of money to communicate this statement—using posters, plaques and newsletters, to name a few methods—but perhaps they do not spend enough time explaining why the statement is important, how it will be used and how it will impact the organization as a whole. We have found that small focus groups or town hall-type meetings are most effective forums for this. It is also important to walk through this with your customers, either through special meetings/forums or one-on-one sessions. Lastly, senior management, creators of this vision statement, must visibly show their support for it. They must walk the talk and demonstrate to employees that this statement truly guides the organization in its current and future direction. They must reward and motivate those that follow this practice and continuously show visible support in speeches and other communication vehicles.

GETTING STARTED

In building a CRM vision, there are four key phases that must be considered:

1. Assess Current Business Context
2. Create the Strawman Vision
3. Build the Business Case
4. Prioritize, Plan and Transform

1. Assess Current Business Context

One of the first steps in the process is to examine both the external market and competitive environment. Within that context, the organization's current business strategies and competencies must be assessed. Is the organization capable of addressing customer needs, and if not, how large is the gap? This will help with the early definition of the current customer segments, relationships and profitability set against the external CRM landscape.

In this phase, it is important to assess the organization's currently articulated customer strategy (not necessarily its CRM strategy), its competitive environment and existing market segmentation. Unfortunately, most organizations have little appetite for this stage. They really do not want to look at where they are now and establish the baseline. They prefer to get on with it and implement some technology—quickly. This is why the assessment is usually rushed. That is a serious mistake. This phase should be based heavily on extracting information from existing data sources, company information and research. That is then augmented through internal interviews and workshops with senior management of the organization, which in addition to providing market and competitive information, also provides insight regarding management expectations, strategic priorities, level of commitment and a management view of how the organization is able to optimize the customer experience. All formal and informal statements of future intent should be captured and recorded because, although these are not reported at this stage, they are an important input to the executive visioning phase of the project.

One key element, and this will be expanded upon in the next section of this book, is the need to conduct a voice of the customer (VoC) survey to obtain a quick view of the customer experience from his or her perspective. Experience shows that it is likely to be a daunting task since it involves setting up interviews with senior managers in client organizations. It therefore needs to be set up as soon as possible after mobilization. A critical success criterion for the VoC survey and analysis is consistency of interview approach to provide comparable feedback. In other words, all interviewers should use the same interview guide and have the same degree of objectivity. VoC surveys are therefore most successful if they are conducted by trained outside consultants, and not by corporate employees.

It is important to keep the data gathering and analysis focused on issues with a significant impact on CRM in order to ensure that the team can complete a robust, fact-based analysis in the time available. Keep the following in mind throughout this phase:

- What are the organization's current CRM practices?

- Are CRM-related business objectives and strategies understood throughout the organization?

- What are the business and management requirements and constraints with regards to CRM? Are all customers to be treated in a similar fashion, or are some customers more valuable than others ?

- Does senior management understand the competitive environment?

- What are the key business drivers that may change the CRM landscape that the company is operating in?

Your analysis should allow you to address the following:

- Environmental drivers, external influences for CRM

  – external environmental forces
  – expected impact of changes in external environmental forces
  – how the organization operates under and reacts to external forces
  – organizational enablers and inhibitors of change
  – issues and opportunities associated with external environmental forces in the context of its ability to react to external forces

- Corporate and functional level strategies as they link to CRM and current operating plans

  – current customer segmentation
  – the organization's understanding of customer requirements
  – current CRM measures of performance
  – customer drivers of value from the perspective of the organization
  – current vision, mission, operating plans and budget

- Competitor analysis of market position and CRM capabilities
  - competitor strengths and weaknesses
  - competitor relative financial position
  - competitor analysis
- CRM partnerships and alliances
  - suppliers and strategic business partners and alliance objectives
  - key organizational interfaces
  - issues and opportunities associated with supplier/business partner interfaces
- CRM organizational issues
  - organization map showing business units, services, locations and people
  - CRM governance
- Measurements and rewards (capability)
  - organizational performance management
  - alignment of individual and team performance metrics and rewards to CRM objectives
  - effectiveness of incentive structure in delivery of CRM objectives
- CRM financial baseline
  - High level churn analysis
  - Cost of CRM organization: cost of customer acquisition, cost of customer retention, cost-to-serve

In addition to the above, it is important that the capability of the organization to manage customer interactions across multiple channels and media is assessed. Channels (Internet, kiosks, mobile capabilities or even interactive TV) should not be introduced if the organization cannot maintain them with competent staff and support systems.

Therefore, you must consider the following:

- both current and future channels
- differentiation of access to channels for various customer segments
- ease of access to the existing channels
- differentiation and personalization of the customer experience

- the extent to which the organization understands and reacts to what customers need and expect across all touch points (customer, front-line employee and management perspective)
- how the organization is aligned to meet customer expectations

At the end of this phase, you should then be in a position to create a CRM business context summary, including:

- the case for change
- evaluation of current CRM business context covering market and competitive environment, CRM strategy assessment and CRM business objectives
- detailed customer analysis (customer expectations, major segmentation characteristics and profitability, competitor positioning)
- financial baseline

2. Create the Strawman Vision

This phase establishes a shared vision of the future of performance driven CRM in the organization among the organization's senior stakeholders and starts the process of communicating that vision to those who will be impacted by the change. This CRM vision should help the organization to understand the following:

- Which customers should they target?
  - All customers do not have the same current and potential value.
  - Not all customers value a complex relationship.
- How should they deal with rapidly increasing channel fragmentation and media complexity to converse with their customers?
  - Rapid changes in delivery channels and new media (e.g., eCommerce) are dramatically increasing the challenges facing both the enterprise and the customer.
- How should they balance quality of experience, cost-to-serve and profitability of the customer?
  - Maintaining highly personalized relationships with all customers is expensive and the 80:20 rule applies (80 percent of profits are derived from 20 percent of customers).
  - Profitability depends on achieving a level of personalization that is both effective and cost effective.

- What is the appropriate level of CRM integration for their business?
  - It will vary with the transactions and types of relationships that they will have with their clients.
  - Integration across channels, media, front and back office systems, functions or business units is expensive.
  - Justifiable integration should be the goal.
- What is customer "insight," and how can the organization get and use it? Which information do they need, and where do they get it in order to continuously update the segments, perceptions, needs, delivery/access channels desired by customer and the company's channels to deliver?
- What should they do with unprofitable customers?
  - Who are they, how should they be dealt with and, should they deal with them at all?

The CRM vision, should contain a specific time horizon and an articulation of the following questions:

- Why do we need to change (strategic and market justification for the vision)?
- Who will our customers be?
- How will we serve them?
- What will be the benefit for us and them?
- What will the future customer experience look and feel like from their perspective?

3. Build the Business Case

This phase provides a structured, repeatable process that aids in achieving and measuring value of the CRM transformation and to build a business case to provide justification for the transformation of the organization. This phase is important because it allows the organization to understand the value of the transformation to itself and its customers, and it builds momentum for change at all levels in the organization.

Here are the key components of the business case:

- Business rationale—Why must the project be done?
- Cost to get to benefits—What are the costs of the change program?

- Payback case (ROI)—What is the overall financial impact measured in payback period, discounted cash flows or internal rate of return?
- Risk analysis—What are the areas of risk and the possible impact of failure, and how are the risks to be managed?

Traditional return on investment (ROI) valuation methods, such as discounted cash flows (DCF) or internal rate of return (IRR), should be used to value the individual projects in the overall CRM program. In order to gain a mandate to proceed, it is critical that all the significant elements of benefit have a business owner, someone who is watching over them.

4. Prioritize, Plan and Transform

This phase creates a program of change that consists of a series of prioritized projects and initiatives that will enable the organization to deliver its CRM vision. Each project will have defined scope, staffing requirements and a distinct approach.

Tight coordination with the third phase above of the CRM vision is required since justification for prioritization is based on the relative importance of each activity to help achieve the business case. Therefore it is important to do the following:

1. Identify, validate and prioritize projects that will deliver organizational transformation to support the CRM vision.

    a) Establish projects to support identified programs.

        i)   Define and scope projects.
        ii) Validate that projects address desired capabilities and identified gaps.
        iii) Confirm projects with project sponsors.
        iv) Finalize scope of projects.
        v)   Estimate and cost projects.

    b) Determine and apply prioritization framework.

        i)   Assess prioritization criteria.
        ii) Develop criteria weighting.
        iii) Apply prioritization criteria.
        iv) Summarize scoring.
        v)   Validate prioritization results.

2. Mobilize quick wins (activities that can be accomplished within three months) and implementation of interim solutions (those that may be replaced or discarded when the long-term solution is in place).

3. Define and mobilize a program to deliver the projects as a single, integrated entity, including:

    a) timing/staging of projects

    b) structure, governance and reporting

    c) sponsorship and stakeholder management

    d) implementation road map

    e) benefits tracking

    f) overall costing

4. Lastly, it is important that you create a CRM transformation program definition document including:

    a) prioritized list of defined CRM projects

    b) future CRM governance

    c) implementation road map

    d) project and program plans (milestone plans with activity level plans to first milestone)

    e) resource requirements

    f) estimated cost

    g) estimated time frame for execution

    h) expected benefits

    i) fit into overall CRM program and CRM vision

    j) alignment to business objectives

That's it—and you thought that CRM vision was just a statement that is put on a wall!

SUMMARY

A CRM vision has two key outcomes: a desired end state and a path to get there. It should provide both a program of projects to deliver against the strategic vision of the organization (a transition and prioritization plan) and a framework to evaluate whether other investments add to and deflect from the net benefits to be realized. It is important that a CRM vision should provide a framework for those solutions that ensures they are compatible with other initiatives and with the strategic direction of the business. A CRM vision should clearly articulate the answers to the following questions:

- With which customer groups do you want to have a relationship, and what type of relationship should it be?

- What does a relationship with these customers mean, and how should it differ with different customer groups?

- What will a "day in the life" of your customers be like from their perspective?

- What will the benefit of the relationships be to you and to your customers?

- How can you make this vision real within your organization?

But, most importantly, it must address the following questions:

- Where are you today? This is the "as is" state.

- Where are you going? What will the end state be 18 months down the road, and what is the business case for change?

- How are you going to get there? What are the major gaps in focus, process, technology and people competencies, and what prioritization must be established in creating the transition plan?

This chapter is a refresher for those who have already embarked on the path to CRM and an introduction for those who have not yet started their journey. But before venturing too far, consider the myths and the facts that follow in Chapter 2.

The Myths and the Facts Surrounding CRM

A CRM vision alone will not ensure success, but it will give you a good head start. But before you embark upon this journey to performance driven CRM, you may need another tool, the one that will help you to fend off those that do not believe in the values and benefits of CRM. The four following myths should strengthen your tool kit.

Let's start by setting the record straight and through this, provide you with the insight to develop, implement and maintain lasting success through performance driven CRM.

MYTH #1: CRM HAS NOT BEEN SUCCESSFUL— IT JUST DOES NOT WORK

Fact:

Let's face it. In many cases, CRM has not been a roaring success, but that is not because CRM, as a concept or strategy, has failed. Generally, it is because senior managers have not been structured in their approach to it and are going about it in a helter-skelter fashion rather than in a performance driven one. Too often, CRM is just not on their radar screen; they appear to be paying lip service to it and probably do not understand what it really is.

Look at this headline from a respected technology research group: "META Group Predicts Serious Risk of Failure for Leading Companies Implementing Customer Relationship Management (CRM) Initiatives." The study, which was based on interviews within the group of 2,000 most significant global companies including Sprint, Nortel Networks, Eastman Kodak Co. and PNC Bank, found that most enterprises do not have adequate CRM business plans and are not spending nearly enough on implementing their CRM projects. The study revealed that most CRM projects are highly fragmented, with no common vision. They are a number of unrelated and competing initiatives. Nor are they customer-centric or customer-focused. META found that most companies underestimate the value of customer information, purchase disparate CRM products and services, focus too heavily on the electronic channel and fail to employ meaningful measurement techniques, a key requirement for performance driven CRM.

Other findings from this study include the following:

- Sixty-four percent of respondents lack techniques to measure the business value of CRM.

- Less than 10 percent of companies are able to measure a tangible return on investment (ROI).

- Less than 30 percent have begun to take steps to integrate operational and analytical CRM environments.

- In spite of marketplace perceptions of the Web—"e-channel"—as a dominant customer contact point, traditional methods (such as face-to-face selling, business partners and the telephone) continue to account for more than 95 percent of revenues.

- Respondents provided multiple, conflicting and often incomplete definitions of CRM. While 78 percent describe CRM primarily as a customer imperative, 22 percent of respondents define it largely as a set of tools and technologies.

That brings us to the next myth.

MYTH #2: CRM IS ALL ABOUT TECHNOLOGY

Fact:

Many organizations do not truly understand what CRM is, how it must be used and who is the beneficiary of this new focus on the customer. They believe that CRM can be achieved through investment in new technology, and the more expensive the hardware or software, the greater customer satisfaction and revenue growth that can be achieved.

Customer Relationship Management (CRM) is neither a concept nor a project. Instead, it's a business strategy that aims to understand, anticipate, manage and personalize the needs of an organization's current and potential customers. It is a journey of change—strategic, process, organizational and technical change—whereby a company seeks to better manage its own enterprise around customer behaviors. It entails acquiring and deploying knowledge about one's customers and using this information across the various points of contact with the customer (known as touch points) to balance revenue and profits with maximum customer satisfaction.

However, CRM is a strategy that must be tailored to each market segment, and therein is the challenge—and the opportunity. To be effective in managing the customer relationship, an organization must define and understand its four strategies:

1. It must define its **customer strategy**. To do that, there must be an understanding of customer segments and their needs. This is a mandatory requirement if one is to understand which products and services to offer for each segment.

2. It must create a **channel and product strategy**. This defines how the organization will deliver its products and services efficiently and effectively, ensuring sales productivity and effective channel management. It will help to determine which products and services are necessary to offer to which customers, through which channels. It is not one size fits all for your customer base. Some customers may be favored.

3. It must understand the importance of a robust and integrated **infrastructure strategy**, and this is where technology comes into play. That strategy will encompass not only technology but also organizational structure and organizational competencies. The

infrastructure will support your ability to execute against your customer and channel strategy and your ability to be a business that is easy to do business with.

4. But for those organizations that desire lasting CRM—performance driven CRM—there is one more element that is required: a **performance management strategy** and action plan. That strategy must embrace performance standards and metrics and an all-encompassing performance program. To be effective, the organization will have to prepare a performance program that will track its performance and be capable of alerting the organization to changes that are necessary for continuous improvement.

Technology is a key enabler of CRM, but it is not the true execution of CRM. In the following case study, identify the various elements and sub-strategies articulated above—the customer strategy, channel and product strategy, the infrastructure strategy, and the performance management strategy—and the role that technology plays in CRM as an enabler.

CASE STUDY

Marriot

Marriott has developed a program, called Personal Planning Service, for a select group of customers, which allows it to create personalized vacation itineraries for guests at seven of its resorts and complete the plans long before they arrive. Each time the customer calls and makes a reservation for one of these resorts, the company adds more information to its database, which helps it plan activities based on the customer's requests and preferences. When the customer arrives at the hotel some weeks later, a personal itinerary has been built—requested tee times have been scheduled, dinner reservations arranged and recreation itineraries created. Marriott has found that guests who participate in the program rate their satisfaction noticeably higher than average and spend an average of US$100 per day on services in addition to room charges. They are also more likely to return to Marriott business because they have had a great experience.

Marriott International Hotels has achieved occupancy levels that are typically 10 percentage points or more above the industry average for similar type of properties, and the Personal Planning Service plays no small part in this success. Marriott's results are a vivid illustration of performance driven CRM. It has clearly establish a customer strategy and isolated a key customer segment for differentiated treatment. The product or service is available exclusively to this customer segment—its channel strategy—and as part of its infrastructure strategy, it has used advanced technology to enable the process and aligned the organization behind this. And then, it has taken the next step. In driving toward performance driven CRM, it has a defined performance management strategy with customer satisfaction performance metrics and used them in a way that strengthens customer value and satisfaction. Marriott monitors numerous aspects of the guest experience—such as the reservation, check-in and check-out processes—in order to measure levels of guest satisfaction and take corrective action where appropriate. High levels of guest satisfaction translate into repeat stays that enhance Marriott Hotel profitability.

There is no one product on the market that will magically create CRM; that silver bullet does not exist. CRM requires an enterprise-wide approach to customer care that involves an integration of the front and back office, and it requires the ability to knit together various hardware and software products into an integrated multi-channel environment. It requires a focus on the customer and an ability to learn from each customer interaction. A recent research report by the Gartner Group, a highly respected information technology research organization, states the following:

Competitively differentiating applications for managing prospects, customers, partners and suppliers are becoming increasingly hot areas. Revamping business processes around selling, servicing, marketing, e-commerce and supply chain planning and scheduling will be on the agendas of every CEO and CIO.

The key to achieving success will be to achieve integration end to end, front office to back office. This entails enterprise workflow, purchased applications, in-house legacy applications telephony infrastructure and the Internet. All these products, hardware and software applications, must be integrated into one seamless solution that interacts with the customer and the organization.

MYTH #3: CRM IS JUST A FAD

There is no compelling reason to change—no burning platform. There is no way to identify if you should be concerned about CRM, and more importantly, it will not provide benefits to the organization.

Fact:

Do any of your customers sound like this?

I am sophisticated, much more so than I was a few years ago. I have grown accustomed to better things. I have money to spend.

I am an egotist. I am sensitive and proud. My ego needs the nourishment of a friendly, personal greeting from you. It is important to me that you appreciate my business. After all, when I buy your products and services, my money is feeding you.

I am a perfectionist. I want the best I can get for the money I will spend. When I criticize your products and services—and I will tell anyone who will listen when I am not satisfied—take heed. The source of my discontent lies in something you, or the products you sell, have failed to do. Find that source and eliminate it or you will lose my business and that of my friends as well.

I am fickle. Other businesses continually beckon me with offers of more for my money. To keep my business, you must offer me something better than they do. I am your customer now, but you must prove to me again and again that I have made a wise choice in selecting you, your products, and your services above all others.

I found this quote a number of years ago in a publication on front-line service by a Florida company called Innovative Business Education Inc. The person speaking could be today's typical customer—more demanding, more discriminating, more fussy. Can you afford to disenfranchise them, or are there benefits to attracting these types of customers?

Organizations that have chosen to embark on CRM have been able to achieve both quantitative and qualitative benefits (as you will see in later chapters). Research conducted by PwC Consulting has found the following, depending on your starting point and commitment to performance driven CRM:

Quantitative Benefits of CRM

Revenue Enhancement	Potential Range of Improvement*
• win-back increase	25%–33%
• service and churn decrease	30%–80%
• renewal rate increase	5%–15%
• acquisition/prospect increase	27%–45%
• campaign cycle time decrease	50%–70%
• campaign conversion increase	20%–50%
• cross-sell/up-sell rate increase	3%–25%
• share of wallet increase	3%–25%
• overall retention rate increase	50%–200%
• partners' market penetration increase	3%–5%
• expense per convert decrease	30%–60%
• mailing cost decrease	10%–40%
• marketing overhead decrease	8%–10%

---

* These areas of improvement and their ranges are based upon cross-industry best practice CRM results. *Source*: PwC Consulting analysis.

CASE STUDY

West Marine

West Marine is a global provider of recreational and commercial boating supplies. With its 220-plus stores, its mail order catalog and its Web site, it has a presence in more than 150 countries. The company was a very early adopter of the Web, as a cornerstone of its CRM strategy, and it now offers all of its 50,000 products online. In one year, West Marine experienced a 450 percent increase in online sales in one month and a 1,000 percent increase in another month. Currently, sales are increasing at a rate of 550 percent annually. The company has developed an alternative customer set but has maintained its older, more traditional distribution system and has linked the two to achieve substantial quantitative benefits through CRM.

Qualitative Benefits of CRM

- more profitable **customer relationships** for the benefit of the enterprise
- increased **operational efficiencies**
- ability to **model customer behavior** across business units
- enhanced marketing, product and channel programs through the use of **better customer data**
- ability to **identify and prioritize** a range of CRM projects across business units
- improved efficiency in **targeting prospects**
- improved efficiency in **marketing communications**
- ability to develop **a strategic investment plan** that specifies expected returns through targeted investments
- **superior alignment of scarce resources** with enterprise-wide strategic initiatives

MYTH #4: CRM IS SUPPOSED TO BE ABLE TO IMPROVE CUSTOMER SATISFACTION, BUT THERE IS NO EVIDENCE THAT IMPROVED CUSTOMER SATISFACTION IS WORTHWHILE

Fact:

Improved customer satisfaction can achieve benefits. Companies are increasingly looking to customer satisfaction as a competitive weapon because the traditional bases of differentiation—product features, price and distribution—are no longer sufficient. Customers can easily compare prices and features through the explosion of online information. This means that product-based differentiation is difficult because product features can be easily copied. Also, prices can be matched or bettered, as can distribution. Once organizations attain a certain level of manufacturing excellence, there isn't much variability on the product side.

In contrast, factors that "delight" customers, such as excellent customer service, are often difficult for competitors to duplicate for two reasons. First, these factors are built into the organization's business processes and culture and cannot be plucked out and copied overnight. Second, it takes a considerable amount of both time and detailed data to determine precisely which factors drive customer satisfaction.

Consider the following: Research conducted by the US Department of Commerce and the Strategic Planning Institute reached four critical conclusions:

1. Return on sales—Companies that give good service and achieve high levels of customer satisfaction achieve a 12 percent return on sales compared to 1 percent return on sales for companies that give poor service.

2. Share growth—Companies that have higher levels of customer satisfaction than their competition generally achieve a higher market share, attain a stronger perception of quality by their customers and can demand (and receive) a premium price on comparable products or services.

3. Success breeds success—Companies that have focused on employee (internal customer) satisfaction have not only reduced turnover, but have had little or no problem attracting new employees. In addition, they have not had to waste money advertising job vacancies.

4. Positive word of mouth—Organizations that give good customer
    service are known in their communities as companies with which
    to do business. Customer loyalty is strong, and repeat business is
    the rule rather than the exception. Indeed, for the typical company,
    repeat sales account for 70 percent of total revenues. Most organi-
    zations are aware that it costs five to 10 times more to acquire new
    customers than it does to keep current ones satisfied.

    Need more proof? A recent study conducted by the University
    of Michigan found that in one large organization, a 5 percent
    increase in customer satisfaction resulted in improved financial
    performance and an average increase of $3.26 billion in market
    capitalization. From another perspective, increasing customer sat-
    isfaction by 1 percent contributes to a 3 percent increase in market
    capitalization.

SUMMARY

The lists of myths can surely go on, but the critical message is that CRM
can succeed, and significant benefits have been realized. Those that fail
have done so because they lacked an enterprise-wide and holistic view
of CRM. They sought the silver bullet, the magic wand in technology.
But, technology alone is not the answer and never will be, although it
will be a key enabler. To flourish, an organization must realize its
strengths and weaknesses, its vulnerability and its preparedness to take
the steps required to be successful through performance driven CRM.
So before you start on your journey, take the next challenge below by
completing the checklist on the next page.

CHECKLIST: ARE YOU READY FOR PERFORMANCE DRIVEN CRM?

For each of the items, identify the priority (scale of 1-5, the higher the number, the more important) and the degree to which you are practicing the following (again on the same scale of 1 to 5) .

1. **Strategic Positioning:** How important are the following, and how effective are you in each?

	Importance	Effectiveness
• identifying profitable and strategic customers and directing best service to them	1 2 3 4 5	1 2 3 4 5
• attracting new customers and retaining existing ones	1 2 3 4 5	1 2 3 4 5
• increasing each customer's spending through strategic channel usage	1 2 3 4 5	1 2 3 4 5
• leveraging most effective, profitable channels to maximize customer value	1 2 3 4 5	1 2 3 4 5
• cross-selling, and up-selling by leveraging customer knowledge	1 2 3 4 5	1 2 3 4 5

2. **Operational Efficiency and Effectiveness:** How important are the following, and how effective are you in each?

	Importance	Effectiveness
• identifying most costly customers, implementing remedial programs or getting rid of them	1 2 3 4 5	1 2 3 4 5
• assessing all channel opportunities, creating channel synergy and leveraging for customer ownership	1 2 3 4 5	1 2 3 4 5
• reducing the cost and time to serve each customer by being better prepared	1 2 3 4 5	1 2 3 4 5

	Importance	Effectiveness
• serving customers from various channels with consistent, quality information about customer's needs	1 2 3 4 5	1 2 3 4 5
• directing customers to best channel for service or the most profitable one	1 2 3 4 5	1 2 3 4 5

3. **Performance Management:** How important are the following, and how effective are you in each?

	Importance	Effectiveness
• better understanding and reacting to customers through analytics and content	1 2 3 4 5	1 2 3 4 5
• measuring performance of all touch points	1 2 3 4 5	1 2 3 4 5
• maximizing customer value through segmentation and campaign management	1 2 3 4 5	1 2 3 4 5
• directing resources and investments where they have the greatest impact on the customer relationship and the organization's performance	1 2 3 4 5	1 2 3 4 5
• using information and feedback from all channels to improve the overall organization	1 2 3 4 5	1 2 3 4 5
• capturing, managing and analyzing real-time customer actions to better serve the customer	1 2 3 4 5	1 2 3 4 5

Look at your scores. In each section, high priority items (those that are four or higher, should also have effectiveness scores of four or higher). Unless scores are five in both categories, you will not achieve performance driven CRM, and lasting success will elude you.

The chapters that follow will help to improve your scores in all areas.

Part Two

Creating Performance-Driven CRM—The Three Critical Performance Programs: Overview

OVERVIEW

There are three critical performance programs in achieving overall enterprise-wide performance driven Customer Relationship Management (PD CRM). The first program, the Customer Performance Program, ensures an ongoing understanding of the customer. The second one, the Organizational Performance Program, ensures an ongoing understanding of its own organization. The final, third program, the Quality Service Performance Program, ensures an ongoing commitment to continuous improvement in quality service.

Essentially, the three performance programs are a framework that is built on performance measurement and performance management. Performance measurement is the capturing and collecting of performance data, while performance management involves taking this data and using it to make essential changes to your business in the areas of your customer, your organization and your level of quality service. The changes will be substantive and will fundamentally drive CRM change.

To translate your CRM vision into a CRM strategy, you will be required to develop an action plan that details various initiatives that are required to reach your end state—your CRM vision. The initiatives will vary from implementing new technology to potentially hiring new staff or re-skilling existing staff. Generally, the initiatives will be those that encompass customer needs (for example, developing and conducting a customer expectation survey), organizational competencies (for example, hiring new staff focused on managing high-value relationships) and a commitment to quality service (for example, an ongoing quality service certification program). You are now ready to act on performance driven CRM.

The three performance programs make up the performance driven CRM scorecard, which can be considered the "CRM cockpit" of the organization. As with an airplane cockpit, this is from where the organization is flown. The CRM cockpit contains all your signal lights: it tells you when your doing something wrong (red signal light), doing something right (green signal light) or when something might be going wrong (yellow signal light). If the performance driven CRM scorecard is not fully implemented, the CRM cockpit will remain an expensive executive toy and not drive the required change. This means that the performance driven CRM scorecard translates the CRM vision into three specific scorecards (one for the organization, one for the customer and one for quality service). These scorecards should then cascade down to specific responsibility centers within the organizational management structure. More detailed measures are then linked to teams and finally to personal employee objectives.

At the end of the day, the purpose of performance driven CRM is to change the behavior of people (the behavior of the customer, management and staff) and to impact CRM decisions and actions. Rewards are a key influencer of behavior, which is why competency development and employee coaching are important elements to support performance driven CRM (these topics are discussed in further detail in Chapter 10).

If your efforts are meaningful to your customers and organization, you will be rewarded. Your performance driven CRM will enable you to:

- Provide accurate, timely, relevant and a *complete* view of performance towards optimal CRM.

- To monitor and manage your CRM vision leading to effective and efficient CRM initiatives.

- Make decisions or have them taken to the right level.

- Integrate with operational systems (rather than have isolated decisions being made and inefficiencies being created).

- Present one version of the truth (one version of performance reality to everyone).

- Form part of a communication strategy.

- Apply the 80/20 rule to your performance programs. You will not need to wait for perfection; you will begin to see results once you get 80 percent of the program up and running and begin implementation while continuing to build the remaining 20 percent.

- Provide energy and direction toward the implementation of the CRM strategy and vision.

It is the implementation of the scorecards that turns performance measurement into management. When this occurs you are practicing performance driven CRM.

The Seven Most Common Pitfalls that Prevent performance driven CRM from Becoming a Reality

In moving forward with performance driven CRM and the development of your three performance programs, watch for these seven common pitfalls:

1. The *Executive Toy Syndrome*—You design, develop but don't fully implement.
2. The destruction of shareholder value is promoted by measuring the wrong things.
3. The *Best Practice Syndrome*—if you don't get it right, you will not do anything.
4. Development is driven by IT alone.
5. It becomes a reengineered reporting process only.
6. Enterprise-wide common *performance management* application are lacking (more on this in Part Three).
7. The links to human resources (your staff) are missing.

To develop the three critical performance driven CRM performance programs, you must examine and really understand your customer, organization and the concept of quality service. The performance programs must provide you with specific performance data that is required to sustain your CRM vision.

UNDERSTANDING YOUR CUSTOMER

To what extent do you understand the needs of your customers? To what extent do you know if those needs are unique to certain market segments versus your whole customer population? To begin building your Customer Performance Program, you must measure and gain an understanding of your customers, their habits and their likes and dislikes. On an ongoing basis, performance information has to be acquired on:

- who the customers are and their needs
- customer purchasing patterns
- the impact of marketing and/or communication efforts

- the match between services and products and customer needs
- current levels of customer satisfaction

This information should then be used to:

- plot current customer needs, wants and expectations
- predict where customer needs, wants and expectations are growing
- predict future customer needs, wants and expectations

UNDERSTANDING YOUR ORGANIZATION

To what extent is your organization prepared to deliver to customer needs? Does it have the required human and physical resources? Is your organization committed to deliver to your customer needs?

To begin building your Organizational Performance Program, you must assess if you have the right people and skills to make your CRM vision a reality (do you have the right complement of resources and the right skill sets?). Your Organizational Performance Program should provide you with ongoing information on the following:

- Organizational alignment—Do silos exist, preventing enterprise-wide CRM vision to become a reality?
- The level of understanding of the CRM goals and objectives throughout the organization.
- The right infrastructure required to allow the CRM vision to happen—Do you have the right technology in place to allow the organization to deliver against your CRM goals? Are required systems and processes that pave the way to being more customer responsive set up?
- Is your organization able to respond to the services and products customers want and in a manner that they want?
- Your market strategy—Does it capture customer attention? Do marketing efforts support current offerings and align with customer needs?

COMMITTING TO CONTINUOUS IMPROVEMENT IN QUALITY SERVICE

To what extent do you have quality standards established and monitored in a manner that supports an environment of continuous improvement? Having a Quality Service Performance Program would mean that you have:

- established CRM champions—individuals who are accountable to keep the CRM vision alive and well

- embedded customer service beliefs—customer service is a priority and a day-to-day activity for all staff

- the following, which are well defined and developed:

  - Customer service expectations and standards—letting all staff know what the customer needs are and what they should be doing to meet these needs

  - Scorecard—measuring all areas that are important to the customer, not just focusing on one (e.g., cost of service)

  - Customer service surveys—asking customers what they thought of the service and what they want from it in the future

  - Complaint management process—inviting customers to voice all their concerns and then doing something with this information

All three performance programs—Customer Performance Program, Organizational Performance Program and Quality Service Performance Program—should:

- promote and demonstrate CRM accountability by assigning performance owners (those responsible for various aspects of performance)

- assist the organization in making better decisions by providing performance driven CRM information that points them to informed changes

- improve allocation of CRM resources by demonstrating where more people, money and time are needed

- invite continuous improvement by advising where they can do better and where they are leading in CRM practices against benchmarked organizations

To be successful in performance driven CRM, the following objectives must be a priority:

- Have a continuous desire to improve management practices—There has to be a commitment to use the performance information.

- Focus organizational efforts on customer needs, wants and expectations—The customer performance information must pinpoint these needs, wants and expectations.

- Assess progress in meeting needs, wants and expectations—Ongoing customer measurement and monitoring should demonstrate where improvements are being made or where performance gaps exists and action is required.

- Ensure that the information to make necessary and best customer change decisions is available—Performance information has to be timely and relevant, not just a stack of data reports and statistics.

- Drive positive change by:
  - focusing attention on the organization's CRM vision—reminding the organization where it wants to go and where it is heading.
  - providing a positive way to direct efforts of management and staff to meet new CRM goals and new ways of doing customer-focused business.
  - continually improving performance at both the organizational and individual level—involving staff and assisting them to see how they can improve and, in turn, the direct impacts of their improvements on the organization.

The following three chapters provide more detail on the development of the three performance driven CRM performance programs.

Understanding Your Customer —The Customer Performance Program

As we stated at the beginning of this book, in order to achieve lasting CRM, a mechanism is required to measure, monitor and manage CRM in an ongoing manner. performance driven CRM is that mechanism.

It starts with a clear understanding of customers and their needs and requires standards and benchmarks that measure that understanding. What is also needed is a mechanism to create change—change in process, actions, organizational structure and people competencies. Do you understand the needs of your customers? Are those needs unique to certain market segments, or are they representative of your whole customer population? To begin building your Customer Performance Program, you must measure and gain an understanding of your customers, their habits and their likes and dislikes. On an ongoing basis, performance information has to be acquired on:

- who are the customers and what are their needs
- customer purchasing patterns
- the impact of marketing and/or communication efforts
- the match between services and products and customer needs
- current levels of customer satisfaction

This information should then be used to:

- plot current customer needs, wants and expectations
- predict where customer needs, wants and expectations are growing
- predict future customer needs, wants and expectations

Organizations have taken to using a variety of tools and methodologies to gain this understanding. This chapter will deal with the measures and information that have to be gathered (the what and the why), and Part Three will provide a deeper analysis on how these tools (methodologies and software) are used to guide performance driven change.

But before we get started, perhaps a case study of an organization that has established standards and measures and uses them to achieve continuous improvement and lasting CRM—performance driven CRM—may be helpful. This enterprise has made news headlines for its meteoric rise to success and also the decline that followed. But regardless of its financial performance, this organization has many lessons to teach. One of its best in class practices is its focus on understanding the customer.

CASE STUDY

Nortel: The Optical and SONET Division

Nortel is a global leader in telephony, data, eBusiness and wireless solutions for the Internet. One of its business units (the Optical and SONET Division) had developed a customer value and loyalty team that reports directly to the business unit president. This team's structure, methodology and accomplishments are outlined below.

This customer value and loyalty initiative within this division started with a desire to systematically measure customer value and loyalty across its product range and key accounts. The team recognized that at its foundation, it would be necessary to first understand the drivers of customer satisfaction and loyalty and how future purchasing behaviors would be affected by this. But more than anything else, it was necessary for the organization to evaluate customer performance data and implement actions to create customer value.

The Customer Performance Program

Nortel (all references to Nortel are specifically to the Optical and SONET Division) first undertook customer surveys and focus groups with account representatives. These were used to identify attributes that influence customers such as product and service quality, customer relationships and price. Approximately 300 business customers were asked to complete these surveys on a biannual basis, but, wisely, no individual within a company was asked to complete a survey more than once a year.

Nortel sticks to its core competencies and uses third parties to assist in the creation and tracking of the surveys, but it does its own analysis internally. The stated target is to have 95 percent of customers rate "satisfied" or "very satisfied" (with at least 30 percent very satisfied) on the overall top of mind score. Quantitative and qualitative measures are tracked, although more time and effort is spent on quantitative measures, since that is what management has requested. Over time, more qualitative questions will be added to create a better balance.

In an effort to create an enterprise-wide focus, Nortel has established a central database that contains all survey results and account plans, which is accessible to everyone who has contact with the customer and responsibility for those plans. Overall, the process was designed to be simple and easy to administer because Nortel found that customers are more willing to provide feedback when the process is straightforward and demonstrates value. To demonstrate the latter, information sessions and day-long forums are organized, sometimes at the customer site, to discuss results and show how feedback is actually used.

Maintaining Organizational Commitment to the Customer Performance Program

Best practices suggest that support must come from the top and that customer satisfaction must be woven into the fabric of the company. This is no exception at Nortel. Senior management is committed to the concept that there is a linkage between customer satisfaction and customer loyalty. And, it is commonly accepted that every employee will work to satisfy the customer. This is part of the operating culture. To underscore the importance of this initiative, the senior executive team begins its monthly business reviews with a discussion of customer data, identifying action items to assign to cross-functional account teams. The customer value and loyalty incentive program creates awareness and encourages a focus on customer needs and cross-functional cooperation. Even the employee compensation structure is tied to performance.

Communication plays a key role here, and the strategy is designed to create a shared understanding of customer needs and values. One of the key tools used is an internal newsletter that includes testimonials from customers. But the company does not stop there and regularly produces communication briefs for customers themselves.

Focus on Strategically Important Customers

Nortel recognizes that its marketplace is changing rapidly. For example, its top 20 customers in 1999-2000 were only prospects in 1997. As a result, a rigorous segmentation analysis is completed and updated regularly to identify and target the most strategic customers, (this is based on criteria other than just current revenue, including potential revenue and profitability, as well as strategic importance to the company and its product lines). Survey results are used as a starting point to engage these key customers in discussions on their business needs. Following that, customer needs are then aligned to Nortel's business priorities, and then the cycle continues. Customers are made a central part of the process to ensure that plans are aligned to needs and that priorities are established and monitored, followed by active communication. Nortel believes that account teams (consisting of sales, customer service and technical service professionals) are the gateway to their strategic customers, and it goes to great lengths to ensure that its Customer Performance Program both helps its performance and monitors it.

In summary, Nortel Networks has been able to translate the voice of the customer into concrete benefits by integrating customer value and loyalty into the business model. Processes and tools, supported by key success factors, create a strong customer focus throughout the organization.

The processes and tools are used to identify and analyze customer data to measure and evaluate business performance relative to the market. This business intelligence supports strategic planning at the executive and operational levels by accentuating customer trends and behaviors. The information is also used to evolve the value proposition, monitor customer relationships and evaluate employee performance. This positioning ensures that the customer is at the center of the business model and that organizational processes and employee actions are aligned accordingly.

Results

Between 1997 and 1999, Nortel had a four-point increase in customer loyalty and a growth of 5 percent in market share. There was also a four-point increase in product quality and a three-point increase in customer perception of value for money. Other indirect benefits have been realized as a result of the organization's focus on customer value. In January 2000, Nortel Networks was among the first companies to receive the quality certification for optical products. TL 9000 is a new telecommunications-specific standard that defines a single, common set of quality system requirements for the telecommunication industry. Within the certification process, the focus on customer loyalty and value was recognized for being process driven, integrated into all levels of the organization, and supported by metrics to drive ongoing improvement.

GETTING STARTED

The concept of understanding the customer starts with, well, talking to them. This is fundamental CRM, but a step that is so often missed by those that say "of course we know our customers; we talk to them every day." But are we listening to the right customers and to the right conversations? Consider the Nortel example above. What are the fundamentals upon which the Customer Performance Program was built, and what is required to drive increased revenue, operating efficiencies and customer

ast experience suggests that the Customer Performance
(CPP) must have triggers that allow you to take action.

our CPP must allow you to understand and respond to the following:

- Customer Needs—Who are my customers, what are their buying patterns and what are their satisfiers and dissatisfiers? How can I encourage repeat purchases, and how can I better personalize the experience?

- Requirements for Customer Differentiation—Which customers are more important, which add value and with whom do I want a lasting relationship? How can I tell when customers no longer contribute to the value that I require to treat them specially?

- The Need for Change in Channel Preferences and Impact—Which channels are most effective with which customers? Which customers require Web speed, and which need multiple channels to communicate and transact business with me?

CUSTOMER NEEDS

According to Lois Geller, author[1] and president of Mason & Geller Direct Marketing, it's important to start by tapping into information that you already have. You would be amazed at the abundance of information produced throughout your organization. The problem is that it typically resides in islands scattered throughout the enterprise—in departments, branch offices, databases, legacy systems and so on—that don't connect, don't speak the same language and just don't mix. But before you pay hundreds of thousands of dollars to connect them all, start by answering some basic questions:

- What are all your current sources of information? Take an inventory and list them. Get the help of your information systems personnel. Know what you have available to you. You may be surprised.

- What do you need to know? Go back a month or two. What was important to you then? What did you need to ask your supervisors, team leaders, branch managers? What reports did you need to produce or get others to assemble?

[1] Lois K. Geller, *Response! The Complete Guide to Profitable Direct Marketing*, New York: The Free Press, 1996.

- How often do you need information? Chances are you need some immediately, but other information is more meaningful when it is stored, analyzed and formatted into reports.

- What is the best way to view this information? Charts may be best for certain types of information, while tabular reports can show totals and summary information. A real-time gauge may be the perfect indicator for certain types of information.

- Who else needs access to it? Do you typically forward information, reports and so on? Perhaps you prepare reports for senior managers or send regular updates on certain performance levels.

- How can this information improve your profitability, revenue, customer service and employee retention?

After you have examined these points, you need to find a vendor who can make this information accessible without having to scrap everything you have and start from scratch. You may need to bring both real-time and historical information together from a variety of disparate systems and databases and present it as a single portal of information right on the PC screen. CRM information can be one of those data sources, sitting right alongside other important data. But look outside your immediate departmental needs. Strong enterprise information portals are what will separate successful businesses from also-rans. (We will see more on portals in Part Three) But whether the information is in a portal or a database, it must allow you to be able to recognize customer needs and take action. Here are seven key areas that must be monitored:

1. Customer Buying Practices

2. Defection Patterns

3. Rewards and Incentives that Have Value

4. Opportunities for Personalization of Offers

5. Appropriate Timing and Frequency of Customer Promotions

6. Effective Customer Retention Programs

7. Actions that Make a Difference

We discuss each of these in turn.

Customer Buying Practices

Build a marketing database and segment it so that you know which customers are buying from you and how much they are spending. It is important to know the number of individual units each customer is buying as well as the dollar volume. Also, know *when* your customers are buying. If everyone seems to be buying in October or November, you can probably conclude that they are purchasing holiday gifts. You can send reminders to your customers saying, "You bought three gift orders from us last year at this time. Is there anything we can do to make your gift giving easier this year?" Your customers will appreciate anything you do to make the buying process easier for them.

Defection Patterns

Have a system in your database that warns you when steady customers have stopped buying. Study your information to see if there's a pattern (if many customers are leaving after a certain period, perhaps you can change your products or services and perhaps enhance them to correct the situation). Talk to your customers, and identify what is causing this dissatisfaction. When customers leave, send them a special offer such as low price or a high discount to bring them back into the fold.

Rewards and Incentives that Have Value

Segment your database, and tie your marketing strategies into the dollar amount your customers spend and their overall profitability potential. Pick your best customers, and talk to them more often. Send them unexpected gifts. Consider a loyalty program such as a frequent flyer (or buyer) program only if you're willing to make a long-term commitment to it. Don't give your customers a special membership program and then take it away after a few months because the administration is too costly or it is too time-consuming. So, if you are going to create a rewards program, be sure it is cost-efficient before you launch it.

Opportunities for Personalization of Offers

Design offers that are targeted directly to your customers. Once you know what they buy from you, you can make offers specific to their buying habits. Suppose I have been buying vitamin E from you every three months for several years. You should send me a targeted offer for a discount on my next purchase of vitamin E along with the opportunity to participate in an automatic shipment program. Tailor your offers to my buying habits, and give me special discounts on things I frequently buy and that are relevant to me.

You can also build one-on-one relationships by having as much information as possible about each customer. Then, if a customer calls to reorder linens for the bedroom, for instance, your telephone representative could say, "Would you like to order the same size linens you ordered last time?" Providing such personal services makes customers believe they are so important to you that you know what they need before they do.

Appropriate Timing and Frequency of Customer Promotions

Study the information from your database, and modify your unique selling proposition to each of your customer groups. Test your mailings over time. If you are sending mailings 10 times a year and getting a low response, try increasing or decreasing the frequency; then measure the lift (or decline) in response.

Companies often continue the same mailing schedule they've followed for years simply because "that's the way it's always been done." What worked in the past may not be working now. There may be more cost-efficient mailing schedules you can follow and get a better response.

Effective Customer Retention Programs

Remember that you are dealing person-to-person, not company-to-person. Everything that you mail to your customers and prospects should sound like it's coming from a human being, not from some inanimate company. And you should be using the same "voice" in all your communications. Your initial mailing, catalog, billing, collection letters and customer retention efforts should all have a tone and style that is uniquely yours. Everything should have the same feel to it. It's not just a matter of consistency. It's a matter of establishing and maintaining a distinctive personality. Any mail that I get from Mrs. Smith's Children Clothing Company, for instance, should reflect that quirky "Mrs. Smith" personality that first attracted me as a customer and keeps me interested.

Actions that Make a Difference

Unfortunately, customers today are almost surprised when they are treated well. People expect to get what they pay for and little else. So if they are treated well, they are going to stick around and keep buying from you. Even small touches like thank-you notes and birthday cards really work well toward overall customer retention. It's easy to send thank-you notes—they can automatically be included with the bill or sent out after the customer has paid.

There have been many studies done on post-purchasing behavior and ways to make your customers happy about the purchase they just made. Many car dealerships send their customers a letter after they buy a car, reinforcing what a good choice they made, how terrific their new car is and that they know they'll get a lot of enjoyment from it. This is an effective customer retention technique because the smarter you make your customers feel about having bought your product, the more likely they are to come back and buy from you again.

Companies are sometimes afraid to send out this after-sale component because they think it gives customers an opportunity to complain. But if there's something to complain about, you should know it so that you can improve your product or service.

REQUIREMENTS FOR CUSTOMER DIFFERENTIATION

At the core of customer differentiation is a recognition that all customers are not the same—some are created more equal than others. In order to build that requirement into the Customer Performance Program, increased emphasis must be placed on the ability to segment customers based on value, rather than the more traditional methods, and to monitor performance and change based on measuring that.

There are many ways to segment your customer base, many of which have been described in our previous books (including *Strategic Customer Care*, Chapter 3), but the real reason to segment is to be able to provide differentiated care on the basis of value. Value in business markets can be defined as the worth in monetary terms of the technical, economic, service and social benefits a customer receives in exchange for the price it paid for a market offering.

Customer segmentation allows you to concentrate on the select few—your strategic customers. These are the ones for whom you want to add value and with whom you can increase profitability (both yours and theirs). It is therefore essential that you use the right criteria and develop the appropriate models for this segmentation exercise. Consider the following criteria when creating customer segmentation:

- willingness to become a partner
- trend of increased revenues generated for your organization
- your current share of customer's business
- potential for this customer to represent a significant share of your organization's business
- significance of your company's product or service to the customer's business
- customers' degree of innovation orientation
- current gross profit achieved from this customer
- potential to cross-sell additional products and services
- current gross profit achieved from this customer
- customer's gross profit potential

In most organizations, data on the last two points is the most difficult to obtain. Customers must be measured on a number of dimensions, including their current profit contribution to the organization and their potential to provide increased profitability in the future. So, if some customers have the potential to buy more of the products that contribute more profit to your organization, it stands to reason that these customers should be encouraged. The challenge is how to identify them and how to use information currently in your database to create a model that can estimate profit contribution and profit potential. In a word, how do you create a customer profitability model?

A customer profitability model is generally a unique development exercise—there is no "one size fits all." But before you set off on the development road, there are a number of lessons to be learned. Organizations within the financial services, telecommunication and utilities sectors have undertaken the most significant amount of work in this area. Those that have been most successful in meeting this particular challenge have essentially developed the ability to tailor and fine-tune their strategies specifically to their most profitable customers.

In an effort to take this to the next level, to protect their investment in customers, savvy businesses concentrate on the time value of customers. They focus on the potential dollar value of repeat and referral business both over time (through the customer's shifts in age, spending patterns and other demographic changes) and over a broad range of products and services. To keep customers coming back, these companies are shifting from transaction-based customer interactions to relationship-based customer interactions. With this approach, over time, customers begin to feel vested in a company and its products. As a result, companies are able to achieve an entirely new level of customer loyalty.

Nortel Networks calls this Return on Relationship (ROR). The business model assumes that change is a constant, including the technology you use to run your business, the products and services you offer the marketplace and the channels you use to market them vis-à-vis the rapid explosion of the Internet as a sales channel. The ROR model also assumes that companies will take a giant leap to incorporate all forms of communication into both their brick-and-mortar and eBusiness models in order to build an enduring relationship with a customer.

Return on Relationship captures a new group of business behaviors that are a requirement for success in today's Internet-charged economy. Implementing ROR strategies requires that companies look beyond customer satisfaction to strive for customer loyalty by focusing on the relationship, not just the individual sale, and by staying one step ahead of their customers' needs and desires. It's a new world where Return on Relationship, defined by how well you foster customer loyalty, will drive return on investment.

By instituting Return on Relationship strategies, companies will be able to understand what their customers are likely to want over time, not just in the context of a single transaction. The heart of the ROR business model is the ability to dazzle customers by creating customer profiles, personalizing interactions and, when appropriate, proactively upselling and cross-selling a broad range of products and services. In every interaction and transaction, customers reveal much about themselves and their buying habits, volunteering information within their individual comfort levels. ROR strategies capture this information and use it to foster customer loyalty by providing a unique customer experience tailored to each customer's specific needs.

THE NEED FOR CHANGE IN CHANNEL PREFERENCES AND IMPACT

To stand out in online and offline business operations, enterprises are using their marketing departments and other resources to support their customer bases, improve customer spending share and acquire new customers. Just because enterprises are now competing at Web speed does not mean they should forget the proven, traditional rules of running a successful business. That is, customers still have channel preferences. And the Web is not the only—nor even necessarily the favored—channel.

Gartner research points out that "Some customers love it [the Web], some do not. Some use it exclusively, while others use it in tandem with other channels. The right approach is not to acquiesce to the futility of uncovering the "right" channel, nor to submit to the illusion that the Web is more art than science, but rather to deploy technologies that extend existing systems to the Web to determine the right offer on the right channels for the right customer at the right time.

Successful enterprises will utilize consistent data about a customer, in every area of the enterprise. In addition, such alignment can enable a company to avoid the cannibalization of its physical stores or operations by its new online presence—or visa versa. By working together, online and offline components can actually complement each other.

Metrics will be needed to assess channel performance, return on investment, customer satisfaction and channel effectiveness (on the sale) and the impact on alternative channels. Monitoring repeat customers is critical. Lastly, enterprises must balance the need to execute on customer data while, at the same time, respecting customer privacy concerns and, of course, the law.

CHECKLIST:
DO YOU UNDERSTAND YOUR CUSTOMER?

Many organizations speak about understanding customers and their needs, but few truly understand what *customers value most*. Take the following test and see how your organization rates.

1. Are your customers' needs clearly defined, and are they regularly updated?

   a. Yes, on a regular basis. It's then communicated back to all staff for discussion and action planning.

   b. Yes, periodically.

   c. No, but we talk about it on an informal basis.

   d. No, not at all.

2. Do you communicate the results of your customer satisfaction surveys regularly throughout the entire company?

   a. Yes, at least monthly through newsletters and posters.

   b. Yes, occasionally, but not as often as we should.

   c. No, but the information is available if anyone wants to know.

   d. No, not at all.

3. Do you actively seek out customer comments and complaints?

   a. Yes, with several methods: formal surveys, customer panels, toll-free numbers.

   b. Yes, occasionally, but not as often as we should.

   c. No, but we respond if there are complaints.

   d. No, not at all.

4. Do you use multiple ways of obtaining customer information?

   a. Yes, we communicate in several ways with our customers, including surveys, focus groups and face-to-face interviews.

   b. Yes, but we could do a better job of it.

   c. No, not enough. We could do better.

   d. No, but I'm sure they are few and far between.

5. Is there a commitment from top management to support the customer-focused service concept?

   a. Yes, and management is good at communicating service goals.

   b. There is commitment, but it doesn't really show.

   c. Management says it believes in it but acts in opposition.

   d. Management doesn't seem to care about service.

6. Do you have a concept of "internal service"?

   a. Yes. We all realize that we must serve one another as well as the customer.

   b. Yes. Most of us think about it at least sometimes.

   c. No. We have a lot of silos in the company.

   d. No. Some people would rather fight than cooperate.

7. Are customers surveyed to determine satisfaction levels for existing services and request for new services?

   a. Yes. They actively survey on both issues.

   b. Yes, I think so.

   c. Sometimes, but we seldom solicit input on requested new services.

   d. No, and they don't care to.

8. Do you have a centralized database for customer information?

   a. Yes, and all staff who need to have access to it.

   b. Yes, but there is limited access to it.

   c. Yes, but there is a lot of customer information on databases kept within departments.

   d. No recognition.

9. Are segmentation strategies clearly defined?

   a. Very clearly. We review customer segmentation constantly and change things if necessary.

   b. Fairly well, though it's been a while since we've thoroughly looked them over.

    c. I don't know. I haven't given it any thought.

    d. Rather poorly. They are bureaucratic and complex.

10. Do you track both customer satisfiers and dissatisfiers?

    a. Yes. This information is used to address continuous improvement.

    b. As well as you can expect.

    c. Not very well.

    d. No. We do a poor job of pinpointing customer issues.

11. Does your company have a spelled-out, easily communicated customer value model?

    a. Yes, and all the staff are aware of it.

    b. Yes, but most frontline employees don't know it.

    c. No, but a model is under development.

    d. No, I'm not aware of one.

12. Do you track channel effectiveness, that is, which channels are most effective in serving the different customer segments?

    a. Yes. We look at cost-to-serve balanced against close rate by channel.

    b. Yes, but we do not communicate this well, or encourage customers to the most effective channels.

    c. Yes, but only periodically, and we do not communicate this well.

    d. No, not at all.

Give yourself four points for every a, three for every b, two for c, and one for d. How did you do?

    Scores of 40 and over indicate a good understanding of the customer and a solid Customer Performance Program. Scores of 30 to 39 show a good foundation, but a need for improvement. Scores of 20 to 29 indicate several flaws and the potential to misread the customer—perhaps too much generalization. Scores below 20 suggest a strong need to establish the fundamentals and rebuild.

SUMMARY

The Nortel example has shown us performance driven CRM in practice and the importance of the Customer Performance Program (CPP) as a foundation program. But having the measures and practices alone is not enough. As we have seen in this chapter, there must be a support mechanism in place to ensure that corrective action is taken, when required, that positive actions are encouraged and that continuous improvement does occur. In Nortel's case, these can be summarized through the following seven key success factors each of which will be discussed below:

1. Executive Commitment to Customer Value and Loyalty

2. Customer Value and Loyalty Is a Key Strategic Performance Measurement

3. Customer Feedback Translated into Concrete Customer Benefits

4. Customer Feedback Disseminated Across the Organization

5. Customer Value and Loyalty Initiatives Driven by Cross-Functional Teams and Partnerships

6. Reward and Compensation Systems Aligned with Customer Loyalty

7. Feedback Process is Simple and Easy to Administer

Executive Commitment to Customer Value and Loyalty

Executive commitment and participation is essential. Nortel's Optical and SONET customer value and loyalty team reports directly to the business unit general manager, illustrating a high level of commitment, endorsement and visibility at the executive level. This commitment also translates to specific actions. Each month, the executive begins business reviews with a discussion of customer data and identifies action items that are assigned to cross-functional teams.

Customer Value and Loyalty is a Key Strategic Performance Measurement

CPP results should be used to assess performance and make decisions. Targets must be set for both customer satisfaction and loyalty. Trends and comparisons are, over time, linked to the corporate compensation strategy. Simply put, a portion of the performance bonus for the account team is linked to customer satisfaction and customer purchase practices.

Customer Feedback Translated into Concrete Customer Benefits

Customers must experience benefits from their participation in the process. Survey results should be used as a starting point to engage customers in discussions regarding their business needs. Customer needs can then be aligned to business priorities with initiatives communicated to customers on an ongoing basis for validation and redirection. If the results of the survey show a level of dissatisfaction in certain areas, then corrective action programs are put in place, discussed with the customer and monitored to ensure that desired results are achieved.

Customer Feedback Disseminated Across the Organization

To transform customer feedback into business intelligence, it is necessary to establish a communication strategy that can create a shared understanding of customer needs and values. Results are discussed and action plans are developed by the account team to ensure that customer satisfaction can be improved and dissatisfiers removed. Each team member understands his or her respective roles. Employees are then able to align their actions to customer requirements.

Customer Value and Loyalty Initiatives Driven by Cross-Functional Teams and Partnerships

The success of the CPP process relies on the proactive use of customer feedback. Improvements can be put in place only when partnerships are established with all functional groups that have an impact on customer value and loyalty. Functional groups take ownership for key actions. Involving employees at the onset of the process—analysis of the information and action planning—is particularly important to encourage employee engagement.

Reward and Compensation Systems Aligned with Customer Loyalty

A CPP creates awareness and encourages employees to focus on customer needs and cross-functional teaming. Results indicate that account teams that participate in the program achieve higher levels of customer loyalty than those that do not.

Feedback Process Is Simple and Easy to Administer

Customers are more willing to provide feedback when the process is simple and demonstrates value. The company also recognizes the value of objectivity and hires external consultants to assist with the survey design and administration. Response rates are increasing and are currently above 50 percent.

Understanding Your Organization —The Organizational Performance Program

How do you know if your organization is ready to take on the challenge of achieving your CRM vision? If all aspects of your organization are aligned and you are able to manage customer information and relationships proactively, then you are ready.

> *Alignment means ensuring that, in order to realize the vision, a strategy exists. All components of the CRM strategy must be focused in the same direction and working together to achieve the CRM vision. All components of the strategy and the organization must also move in the same direction, which has to be clear enough so that without doubt, all individuals know where they are going and how they fit in.*

Is your organization ready to attain your CRM vision? Does your staff understand what they have to do? Are they equipped with the right skills and knowledge? Do you know if they can do it? Do you know if your technology is working for you? Do you know if you are spending your dollars wisely on CRM initiatives? If you answer "no" to any of these questions, you need an Organizational Performance Program.

The Organizational Performance Program provides you with information on how prepared the organization is to optimize and achieve CRM. Figure 4–1 lists the six dimensions that should be taken as a starting point in developing your Organizational Performance Program. A dimension is a major area that you will measure within your Organizational Performance Program. For each dimension, performance measures must be developed. A performance measure is a more detailed description of what you are going to measure (e.g. customer service). Then performance indicators are developed. Performance indicators are the data requirements that indicate your performance within that measure. For example, for the customer satisfaction measure, some of your indicators may be the number of customers out of the total customer base that indicate they are *very* satisfied with your service. Organizations today cannot rely on only one or two dimensions from which to make informed change decisions concerning customers. No single dimension (or even two) can provide a clear performance picture of the critical areas of the organization required to deliver your CRM vision.

Figure 4–1   The Six Dimensions of the Organizational Performance Program

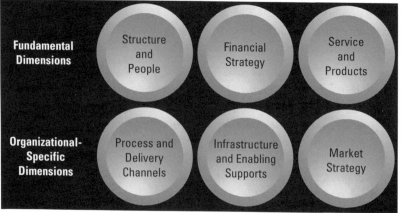

A dimension is an area that will be measured within the program. As a guideline, there are usually a minimum of three dimensions and a maximum of six. The Organizational Performance Program has the highest number of dimensions—usually no more than six. Organizations that have attempted to develop the Organizational Performance Program with more than six dimensions have found it difficult to gain consensus on the dimensions and to implement the program. The number of dimensions is specific to the organization, and the dimension may change depending on the specific type of business. For example, in government, the market strategy dimension may not be necessary, but a new stakeholder management strategy dimension may be important. The three fundamental dimensions for any organization are: Structure and People, Financial Strategy, and Service and Products. The other three are specific to the organization but are becoming fundamental in nature as well. The Infrastructure and Enabling Supports Dimension, and the Process and Delivery Channels Dimension are starting to be consistently used by most organizations. Most often, the Market Strategy Dimension is the only dimension that changes specific to organizational needs. For the private sector, measuring the market strategy is critical and should be included in the program; for the public sector, this dimension may be eliminated or replaced.

In order for the Organizational Performance Program to drive change, it must ensure that each member in the organization has a clear understanding of what is expected and how it relates to the organization's CRM vision and strategy. Members of the organization must understand how their individual influence and performance contributes to satisfying the customer. Setting clear expectations and targets on individual performance as they relate to established performance measures is an important component of the performance process. In Chapter 8, we will review the concept of employee performance agreements and how they can be used to set clear expectations and drive positive change.

THE SIX DIMENSIONS

Your Organizational Performance Program should provide valuable performance data. To accomplish this, specific measures and performance indicators must accompany each of the dimensions. When the measures and data requirements are grouped, they answer the questions listed below for each dimension.

Structure and People

This dimension measures how ready the organization is to meet customer needs. It measures the skill and capacity of staff and how they are organized. Does the organization have the required human and physical resources, and is the organization committed to deliver to customer needs?

Under this dimension, you should ask yourself the following:

- Does your organizational structure support the appropriate roles, responsibilities and authority required to make your CRM vision a reality?

- Is accountability clearly defined (by position), and does it contribute to and enable the CRM vision?

- Where are shifts in staff required, or where are more staff needed?

- Do the right skills, knowledge and capacity exist?

- How committed, loyal and effective are staff?

- Where is performance superior, and where do improvements need to be made?

Financial Strategy

This dimension measures your CRM budget. Are you on target, or are you over or under budget? Are you spending too much too soon or too little too late?

Under this dimension, you should ask yourself the following:

- Have you committed the required amount of money to the right areas?

- Are you spending enough on your people?

- Is your investment in people, process and technology paying off?

- Do you have the appropriate balance in your expenditures?
- Are you meeting your financial targets?

Service and Products

This dimension measures the suitability of your services and products for your customers. How well do the service and products meet and anticipate your customer needs?

Under this dimension you should ask yourself the following:

- Is your organization in the right business to meet your customer needs?
- Do you require expansion or significant change?
- Do your current products and services meet customer needs, wants and expectations?
- Can your current products and services sustain emerging trends?

Process and Delivery Channels

This dimension measures all internal processes, which contribute to customer service, including back, middle and front office. It also measures the various methods of delivering these services to your customers (e.g., phone, web, e-mail, fax, in person).

Under this dimension, you should ask yourself the following:

- Are your processes and delivery channels enabling or inhibiting?
- Are your channels designed to promote creativity, ownership and accountability, or do they stifle it?
- Are they properly integrated while providing the flexibility and customized service levels your customers want?

Infrastructure and Enabling Supports

This dimension measures the internal supports that should be supporting your CRM effort. Both the infrastructure (e.g., technology) and enabling supports (e.g., training programs).

Under this dimension, you should ask yourself the following:

- Can your organization accomplish your CRM vision with what you have now (people, technology, process)?

- Do you have the necessary and required technology, training programs, culture and environment?

- Is your leadership appropriate?

- Do you have CRM champions, not only at the top, but also spread across the organization?

- Do you require additional change levers such as change management workshops, customer service training and new technology solutions?

Market Strategy

This dimension measures how well your advertising is communicating to your customers. Are you reaching them through your various campaigns and grabbing their attention?

Under this dimension you should ask yourself the following:

- Have you targeted your market strategy correctly?

- Is your strategy innovative and creative enough to draw customer attention?

CASE STUDY

FedEx

FedEx is a global transportation and logistics organization that offers a diverse portfolio of solutions, making deliveries by airplane, train or truck. With over $16.7 billion in revenue and 140,000 employees globally, the company is known for its reliable on-time deliveries around the world. FedEx ensures horizontal organizational accountability through an organized network approach to providing customer service. All operational units work as one by balancing workload and resources across three district areas. Service levels are not compromised. Even in a budget-constraint environment, service comes first. Service is a *fundamental* building block for all strategies—everything is built around the organizationally set service levels. FedEx ensures their Organizational Performance Program through the development of a strong customer service culture. All new customer service representatives attend four weeks of training that is primarily focused on knowledge and how to use systems to service customers. Culture is embedded and sustained through a continuation of "great customer service stories," the demonstrated leadership of management and "PSP" philosophy (people/service/profit). The company further embeds the Organizational Performance Program by tying compensation to performance. FedEx has a number of programs that contribute to its Organizational Performance Program. Highlighted programs that enable a performance driven change culture are as follows:

- Survey-Feedback-Action Program—An annual employee satisfaction survey in which staff rate management's performance and offer areas for improvement. Surveys of this nature are often confidential to ensure that employees are not intimidated and provide honest feedback. The survey results form the basis for organizational improvement. In addition, the feedback loop is embedded in this process, as there is a requirement to meet with the employees within 30 days of receiving the completed survey. If the survey is confidential, a different feedback loop must be in place—e.g., a posting of actions taken against the recommendations. This type of program provides critical performance information within the Structure and People Dimension.

- Leadership Evaluation and Awareness Process—An educational program that focuses on the type of leaders required in this organization (leadership qualities such as honesty, trust, openness are focused on and taught). The program must be completed in order to progress to the management level. This type of process provides critical performance data within the Infrastructure and Enabling Supports Dimension.

- Guaranteed Fair Treatment Procedure—This program ensures that any employee who has a complaint is heard. Typically, organizations find that complaints are often around scheduling, how promotional opportunities are handled and the lack of communication around the CRM vision in the organization. This type of program provides critical performance information within the Structure and People Dimension.

- Service Quality Index SQI—This index is a list of what dissatisfies a customer from most to least (e.g., late arrival of a package may dissatisfy a customer the most, whereas the higher price for fastest service dissatisfies the customer least). Service is measured against this list. Where there is a performance gap in an area that would contribute to customer dissatisfaction, the gap is reviewed, and process improvement occurs. This type of process provides critical performance information within the Service and Products Dimension

How does FedEx ensure organizational-wide performance? All internal partners (e.g., all components/management units of the organization) understand that there is a "requirement" to participate and cooperate with one another to satisfy the customer. They follow the philosophy that no one fails or succeeds individually; an entire department succeeds as a unit. In some organizations, to further secure this concept of organizational-wide performance, rewards and incentives are based on how well the entire unit meets its targets, not how individuals meet their targets. For example, if a sales team meets its overall target, everyone on the team is provided with a one-week vacation. If the team does not meet its target, it does not matter how well one employee did. How have they kept organizational performance high? Some of their best practices are as follows:

- Do not accept missed service levels anywhere in the organization—eliminate all the wiggle room, and accept no excuses for poor performance.

- Do not focus on call handle time in call centers. This will drive staff out of the organization and does not conclude in quality performance.

- Focus on quality and the service process. Minimize the focus on the numbers by your frontline employees. Be careful of unintended consequences through goal setting. For example, an employee may be compensated only on units sold. The goal to sell many units may result in the unintended consequence of a "pushy salesperson." If the employee was measured on quality of call and sale process, this type of unintended consequence would not occur.

DEVELOPING YOUR ORGANIZATIONAL PERFORMANCE PROGRAM

Although there are many methodologies in developing performance measures, the key differentiator for the Organizational Performance Program (OPP) is to link measurement to management and then drive change. As stated previously, we define performance measurement as capturing and collecting performance data, while performance management is taking this data and using it to make required and substantial changes. To drive change, a structured approach to analysis and reporting and taking action through the development of improvement plans is required. Training, coaching and management of staff performance is also critical. The following nine steps will provide you with a starting point in developing your Organizational Performance Program.

Step One: Develop the Organizational Performance Program Framework

The framework outlines the principles to be adhered to when building the Organizational Performance Program (e.g., to ensure a minimum level of quality service for all customers from all staff, regardless of position). It further identifies the key customer outcomes (e.g., to ensure no customer experiences the "wrong door," meaning that at any point of contact, the customer will receive the assistance he or she is looking for). Turning this framework into a user-friendly template to assist with the development of the dimensions (major groupings of measures), performance measures (areas that are specifically measured) and indicators (required performance data) will ensure an appropriate level of commonality in the organization regardless of who implements the framework. The template should illustrate how the performance indicators align with the performance measures and how these, in turn, align with the dimensions and performance driven CRM outcomes. The organization will use this template to fill in the definitions for the dimensions, performance measures and performance indicators.

Step Two: Identify Dimensions and Describe How These Will Measure the Outcomes

Once the dimensions have been identified, map them to your performance driven CRM outcomes to ensure alignment. This step is basically determining the relationship between dimension and outcome. For example, your Organizational Performance Program would, at a minimum, include the three fundamental dimensions: Structure and People, Financial Strategy, and Service and Products. You may also chose to include the Market Strategy Dimension and the Process and Delivery Channel Dimension in your program. One of your performance driven CRM outcomes might be *to migrate customers to the most effective service delivery channel available to them through an effective marketing campaign involving the most effective method.* The Marketing Strategy Dimension will provide performance data on the best way to market information to various customer segments. The Structure and People Dimension measures the required skills for the marketing effort and the organizations ability to execute this effort, and the Process and Delivery Channel Dimension measures the usage, effectiveness and cost of each channel. Together, these three dimensions will indicate whether or not the organization has met the performance driven CRM outcome. Figure 4-2 illustrates the alignment of the dimensions and performance driven CRM outcomes.

Figure 4–2   The Performance Driven CRM Outcome

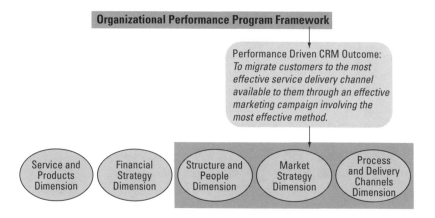

Step Three: Create a List of Performance Measures and Performance Indicators that Will Determine If the Dimension Is Meeting the Performance Driven CRM Outcome

At this point, measures are not evaluated, creativity is encouraged and all ideas are captured. Although many of the measures created in this step will not be used in the long run, the process often helps to identify newer and more effective ways to measure important elements that lead to better performance information. To help you begin your list, identify what needs to be measured, what kind of measurement information is currently available and what measurement information is not available.

Continue with the previous example, within the Market Strategy Dimension, the required performance measure may be (only one example):

- the number of customers who move to a more effective/efficient channel and remain there for over six months

The supporting performance indicators for this measure may be as follows (not an exhaustive list):

- the total number of potential customer contacts that could be made (e.g., 50,000)

- the number of contacts actually made to customers (e.g., 40,000)

- the number of positive contacts made—customer response indicates that customer will move to desired channel (e.g., 20,000)

- the length of average time for customers to migrate to a new channel (e.g., two months)

- the number of customers who migrate back to the original channel in less than six months from the date of migration (e.g., 5,000)

Step Four: Assess the Feasibility of Each Performance Measure

In this step an evaluation tool that will assess the list of measures against critical criteria for your organization should be developed. Each criteria should also be assessed for the relative importance in the overall evaluation. For example, the accuracy of data is often the most important criteria—more important than cost. Suggested criteria to use are as follows:

- Validity—Is the measure appropriate?
- Controllability—Does it relate to factors that management could directly affect?
- Clarity—Is the measure clear and understandable?
- Accuracy—Is it reliable and can it be confirmed?
- Cost—Does the benefit of collecting the data outweigh the cost?
- Timeliness—Can it be collected and processed within a useful time frame?
- Consistency—Does it relate to the same factors in all cases, at all times?
- Accessibility—How easy is it to collect the information?

At this stage, it is also necessary to ensure the following:

- Consistent terminology is being used.
- Only information that is needed to paint a picture of performance is to be collected, and so unnecessary information will not be collected and effort will not be wasted.

Step Five: Define Performance Measurement Attributes

The attributes, or characteristics, describe the important features of the performance measure. They describe what the measure is going to measure, who the measure belongs to—for example, who can make changes to the definition and how often data will be collected for the measure. Specifically, the attributes that define and explain the measures include the following:

- The Definition—What will this measure determine? What was the rationale for choosing the measure? The definition should also state whether this will be a regularly used measure or only used for ad hoc analysis.
- Who Is Accountable—Who *owns* the measure? The owner is accountable for the integrity of the performance data and the upkeep of the definition. He or she approves any changes.
- The Data Source—This provides the details details from where the data come (e.g., an external or internal source).

- Collection Interval—This provides information on the frequency of collection (e.g., monthly, quarterly, annually). A statement should be included to define how often the data is required. Never overcollect data; this leads to inefficiencies and wasted costs.

- Data Type—This includes surveys, tables, etc.

- Weighting—This is the relevant importance of the measure as compared to the other measures in the dimension.

- Influencing Factors—This includes environmental conditions over which the organization has little or no control but which can affect performance (e.g., the economy).

Step Six: Determine the Baseline, Targets and Standards for Each of the Performance Measures

Using benchmarking and historical data, identify the baseline (the starting point to which you will compare), the standards that must be reached, short-term targets and long-term stretch targets. Setting targets lays the foundation for continuous improvement. For example, the standard may be to respond to customer complaints within 24 hours, the short-term target is to respond within 12 hours, while the stretch target—the optimal level of performance for the future—is to respond within five hours.

Step Seven: Define a Regular Reporting Process

For each dimension, and perhaps measure, determine how to report and to whom. The frequency of reporting should also be determined— e.g., monthly, quarterly, yearly. Some dimensions may be a yearly report, with a group of supporting measures as monthly reports. For example, you may report to senior management on a monthly basis on all the dimensions, to frontline staff on a weekly basis all the dimensions and performance measures and to your customers on a yearly basis on only two of your dimensions. Develop a consistent format to allow easy comparison with previous reports. The format, content and reporting interval will generally depend on the audience and its information needs. It is important to demonstrate early success, regardless of the reporting system, by providing examples of how performance information is being used.

Step Eight: Take Action

Based on the information acquired through the analysis of performance measurement data, the organization should now be in a position to do the following:

- Ensure that is heading in the right direction.

- Determine if more or less performance information is required in a particular area.

- Identify areas that have not been meeting the standards, and develop a strategy to assist improvement.

- Identify areas that are exceeding the standards, perhaps meeting the target or, in some cases, the stretch target. These areas often have found a best practice that has allowed them to excel. Identify this practice, and implement it where applicable across the organization, driving positive change.

- Determine if new standards, new targets and stretch targets will need to be set.

- Make resource (people and financial) decisions.

Step Nine: Practice Performance Driven CRM

Practicing performance driven CRM means taking the performance data your program is providing and using it to continuously to improve your CRM efforts and move towards your CRM vision. With the performance data from each of your dimensions, you now have the ability to do the following:

- Affect management—Change the way the organization is managed, instil new and creative ideas and banish the old methods that are no longer getting the job done.

- Demonstrate performance—Communicate internally and externally. Show where you are exceeding customer expectations. For example, release a regular (monthly) customer performance newsletter to staff, or release a semiannual report to your customers indicating how the organization has met customer expectations.

- Excite and drive change—By demonstrating performance, identifying/implementing internal best practices and making appropriate resource decisions, staff will see the commitment to performance and will follow suit. Encourage staff input, comments, complaints and superior performance with a well-developed integrated feedback loop and reward system.

- Continually improve—Never stop at meeting the standard. Always move up the ladder to your target and eventually your stretch target.

CRITICAL ELEMENTS IN DESIGNING YOUR ORGANIZATIONAL PERFORMANCE PROGRAM

Following the nine steps outlined in this chapter will help guide you in the development of your program. In addition, the following seven critical elements must be a part of your development process to ensure success at the end.

1. Ensure that measurement is tied to meaningful performance driven CRM outcomes (outcomes that your customers care about such as high-quality service). Otherwise, you may make decisions based on performance data that is not relevant to your customers.

2. Measure critical components and the end deliverable, and do not focus on measuring the end-to-end activities such as detailed components of a two-day staff training. What is important to measure is what impact the training had, not how many attended and the level of participation. Measuring end-to-end activities will result in *overmeasurement,* which will slow down the process considerably with little gain.

3. Clearly document and agree upon definitions. The entire organization will then understand what is being measured. This will ensure that in the end, apples are compared to apples.

4. Internal performance data and comparative benchmarks should be used to establish standards and targets.

5. Measures should be objective, not subjective.

6. Use a traffic light or cockpit system (red, yellow, green) to easily communicate performance.

7. Make sure that what you measure your employees on is aligned with your Organizational Performance Program (OPP). This will ensure that employees are being measured on what is important to your customer.

Once you have developed your OPP, test your program with the following nine questions. If you answer "no" to any of the questions, stop and rethink your OPP.

**Nine Questions To Test Your Organizational
Performance Program**

	Yes	No
• Is the organization's performance managed through a sufficiently balanced set of financial and nonfinancial measures?	❏	❏
• Do the measures reflect the CRM vision and strategy well enough?	❏	❏
• Are the measures cascaded consistently to management units throughout the organization, to the individual level?	❏	❏
• Do the performance measures reflect the behavior required of staff and enable the CRM vision to happen?	❏	❏
• Are the key elements of the Organizational Performance Program sufficiently integrated with business planning, financial management and personal/team behavior/rewards?	❏	❏
• Overall, does the performance information provide a good enough picture of how the organization is doing and what it will need in the future?	❏	❏
• Is the best use made of the performance information that is already available today? Is it clear, consise and accessible?	❏	❏
• Is corrective action taken when it is needed and at the level it is needed, to keep the organization on track?	❏	❏
• Does the program drive change?	❏	❏

A successful Organizational Performance Program that enables performance driven CRM should result in all positive responses. Your OPP should have a minimum of the three fundamental dimensions: Structure and People, Financial Strategy and Service and Products. Each dimension should then have a number of performance measures and indicators that when analyzed, demonstrate how well you are achieving your performance driven CRM outcomes and your CRM vision. Your performance measures should be feasible and have detailed definitions and clearly articulated attributes. A baseline, targets and standards for each of the measures must be determined in order to measure against these. Otherwise, how will you know how you are doing? With your Organizational Performance Program developed you are ready to design a reporting process, take action and practice performance driven CRM.

Committing to Continuous Improvement in Quality Service —The Quality Service Performance Program

It's simple—quality service (QS) leads to very satisfied customers, to loyal customers, to increased revenue. Some organizations have found that providing quality service is dependant on having the right people, tools and training. These same organizations have also found that providing quality service is much different than *consistently sustaining* quality services throughout the organization to all of their customers. An organization that is committed to quality service will actually drive customer expectations up. Its customers will come to expect more and more from this organization. In meeting these growing expectations, customer loyalty increases. It becomes very difficult for another organization, which does not know these customers as well, to meet their expectations in the same manner and same high-quality service as your organization does.

It does not matter what business your are in—whether it is high-end retail or low-end retail, whether it is the automotive industry or the financial industry—customers want their expectations met. Customer expectations may differ depending on the industry or value of product being purchased; it is therefore critical to understand your customer expectations and definition of quality service relative and specific to your business. Once understanding this, it is then critical to understand if your organization can deliver on these expectations and definition of quality service.

Your customers may differ—you will have some that are more important than others, more valuable—however, all should receive quality service regardless of what segmented group they are in. They will receive different levels of service, different types of service and perhaps even have different service delivery channels (the method in which you serve your customer, such as by phone, in person, through the Internet, etc.). Yet all of them expect quality when they get service.

The only way to sustain quality service consistently is by building and implementing the third performance program—the Quality Service Performance Program (QSPP). By investing in the QSPP, the organization demonstrates a commitment to continuous improvement in quality services and sends a message loud and clear to all staff that this is the number one priority for customer service. It is not good enough to just do well—you have to do better.

CUSTOMER LOYALTY

The link between customer satisfaction, customer loyalty and increased revenue has been studied and proven by numerous organizations. For example, the findings in Table 5-1, taken from research completed by Naumann & Associates, demonstrates that very satisfied customers stay with an organization (are loyal) at a much higher rate than very dissatisfied customers. For example, of those customers who gave a very satisfied rating (5 points), 92 to 97 percent of them were still customers a year later.

Score (5-Point Scale)	Average Retention Rate (1 Year Later)
5 Very Satisfied	92%–97%
4 Satisfied	80%–85%
3 Neither	60%–65%
2 Dissatisfied	15%–20%
1 Very Dissatisfied	0–5%

Table 5–1

The startling finding from this research is that even satisfied customers are leaving at a rate of 15–20 percent. Table 5-2 does the math for you for a fictitious organization with a customer base of 100,000 and an equal distribution of scores from their total customer base (e.g., 20,000 customers fell into each rating category).

Rating	Total Customers Out of 100,000	Customers Lost
Very Satisfied	20,000	600–1,600
Satisfied	20,000	3,000–4,000
Neither	20,000	7,000–8,000
Dissatisfied	20,000	16,000–17,000
Very Dissatisfied	20,000	19,000–20,000
TOTAL		**45,600–50,600**

Table 5–2

Clearly, the math shows that there is cause for concern when even satisfied customers are leaving. Losing customers amounts to losing revenue. If we assume, for the purpose of this example, that each customer is of equal value (revenue), then 50 percent of revenue is lost each year. To make up this revenue, new customers must be attracted and revenue must be driven up for existing customers. One other way of sustaining revenue is to move some of the satisfied customers and even the customers who are neither satisfied nor dissatisfied into the very satisfied category since this category has a lower abandonment rate. Of course, to do this type of analysis, you must first know your current customer base and complete satisfaction surveys. To improve on the ratings, you must first ensure that you know your organization and if it is in a position to deliver quality service.

However, to really be able to capture the attention of your customers and keep it, the quality service your organization is able to deliver has to improve continuously. Customer expectations increase, and competitor's quality service efforts are increasing as well. To stay ahead of your customers and ensure that you are always providing quality service and moving your customers up the rating scale to the point where you actually decrease the number of very satisfied customers who are currently leaving (since you will be delighting them and receiving an over-the-top rating), you must commit to a process of continuous improvement in quality service. However, what your customers call quality service one day is not the same the next day! Your organization must be ready to respond to these shifting customer demands. To be able to respond you must first be aware of the changes. A strong Customer Performance Program (CPP) will measure these shifting demands, a strong Quality Service Performance Program (QSSP) will measure if you are meeting these shifting demands. Without a CPP and a QSPP, you are most likely expending resources (time and money) on servicing customers but are no longer meeting their demands. This leads to dissatisfied customers who, in turn, abandon your organization, leading to lost revenue.

The case study that follows demonstrates how commitment to quality service can ensure ongoing customer loyalty.

CASE STUDY
USAA—Building Customer Loyalty Through a Commitment to Quality Service

USAA is an insurance and diversified financial services association with over US$6.5 billion in revenues and approximately 20,000 staff. The company has about 3 million customers, with the majority of service provided through contact centers. It has been servicing present and former members of the US military and their families since 1922. Although open to all people, the majority of its customer base is military personnel and their families. They are one of America's leading insurance and financial services companies and are well known for their exceptional service. USAA's unwavering dedication to member needs and service helps set high standards for excellence in the financial services industry. Care and attention is given to helping each and every member. Most of the service is provided through contact centers; however service is also provided by fax, the Internet or in person.

USAA has developed a strong trust and loyalty culture with their customer group by putting customer service first. The company involves its customers in decision making on issues concerning service and have a very high return rate on any customer surveys the organization conducts. The reason for this is that the firm has a strong feedback loop to its customers, which indicates how their input was incorporated. The company's mission statement articulates that service to customers comes first and foremost: "USAA seeks to be the provider of choice." The enterprise has a strong and visible customer service and performance culture and is focused on performance measurement and remedial action when required. All staff members are aware of their contribution and how they fit in. This is accomplished by reporting back to all employees both positive and negative customer feedback. All employees involved in servicing the customer (either through direct customer contact or not) are aware of how their actions contribute to high-quality service. If any customer is dissatisfied, every employee involved in providing the service contributes with suggestions of how the service can be improved. USAA measures customer service on a daily, weekly and monthly basis. Any deviation from the targets and goals are scrutinized, and action is immediately taken (at times, on a daily basis).

USSA credits its ability to maintain customer loyalty to four main critical success factors:

1. sustaining a strong customer quality service culture

2. aligning the organization so that all staff members know how they can contribute to quality service

3. having detailed accountability that is followed up on

4. measuring the right things and acting on them (e.g., what is important to the customers)

Some of the ways that USAA has embedded its strong QSPP culture and its commitment to continuous improvement is through:

• *Strong accountability, which trickles down to the front line.* If the organization receives a complaint letter addressed to the president of USAA, every staff person involved with that customer, anywhere in the service chain, participates in identifying methods of improvement.

• *Clear performance objectives to which individual areas are held accountable for.* In addition to being accountable for their individual activity and performance, staff members are expected to contribute to the overall performance objective and for determining what course of action is to be taken if the overall performance objective is in danger of not being met.

- *Rewards and compensation are directly tied to meeting individual performance objectives and overall USAA performance objectives.* Staff members receive monetary and nonmonetary rewards (recognition) for meeting both their own performance objectives and those of USAA.

- *An employee feedback loop, whereby employees provide feedback to the organization on a voluntary basis.* All employee suggestions are acted on, and this promotes and encourages additional employee input (over 80 percent of employees respond to the voluntary employee satisfaction survey).

- *"Tiger Teams," which are specialized teams that come together to resolve a problem or solve a performance gap.* Team membership is based on a specific performance gap such as a delay in service due to an existing process. The team is brought together if a performance target is outstanding for more than one month.

- *Not simply focusing and measuring efficiency, but making the phrase "service comes first" a reality.* This organization believes that if you provide quality, timely, accurate and reliable service and satisfy your customers, efficiency and profitability will follow.

- *Conducting regular performance measurement.* USAA measures performance on a daily, weekly and monthly basis, with formal reporting for each of these time periods. The daily reporting is used to manage the customer-facing staff and is usually only used by frontline management, and weekly reports are reviewed by middle management. The monthly reporting is reviewed by senior management. Most performance gaps are corrected through the daily and weekly performance reviews. Those that are not are highlighted on the monthly report, and the appropriate corrective action is then decided on by senior management (e.g., bringing together a Tiger Team).

- *Trending and forecasting future targets using performance information.* If current targets are being met easily, they are adjusted upward. For example, if your target was to provide quality service (as rated by your customers) 75 percent of the time and you were at 80 percent, you might revise your target to 85 percent. In addition, the firm strives for continuous improvement by raising the bar each year. Each year, USAA attempts to do better than the previous year.

- *Measuring the end deliverable and then looking to the process and activities for improvement opportunities.*

HOW TO CREATE CONTINUOUS IMPROVEMENT THROUGH A QUALITY SERVICE PERFORMANCE PROGRAM

The foundation must be built that positions the organization as "the standard for quality" that others want to model themselves after. Those organizations that are most successful in maintaining the quality endeavor are the ones that have a well-defined Quality Service Performance Program based on a commitment to continuous improvement. Your program must give customer service a priority, making it a day-to-day activity for all staff.

Commitment to continuous improvement in quality service does not automatically flow from an existing CRM vision or a good understanding of the customer and organization. To ensure that this commitment is sustained, a QSPP is required. Traditional programs that focused on quality and continuous improvement are often not directly related to the CRM vision, nor are they an integral part of the two other performance programs. These types of programs focus on management of staff much more than continuous improvement in providing quality customer service based on customer expectations. This focus is the foundation of a Quality Service Performance Program.

The Quality Service Performance Program route map (see Figure 5-1 on page 88) outlines the key steps to achieving optimal quality service. Although your program will vary depending on your specific circumstances and how much you have already implemented in regards to a QSPP, the following route map can act as a guideline for initiative start-up or as a validation of your current program. Steps One to

Four must be completed sequentially. Steps Five, Six and Seven may be completed at the same time, and Step Eight is required throughout the development process. Each of these steps is discussed in turn.

Figure 5–1 Quality Service Performance Program Route Map—Eight Steps

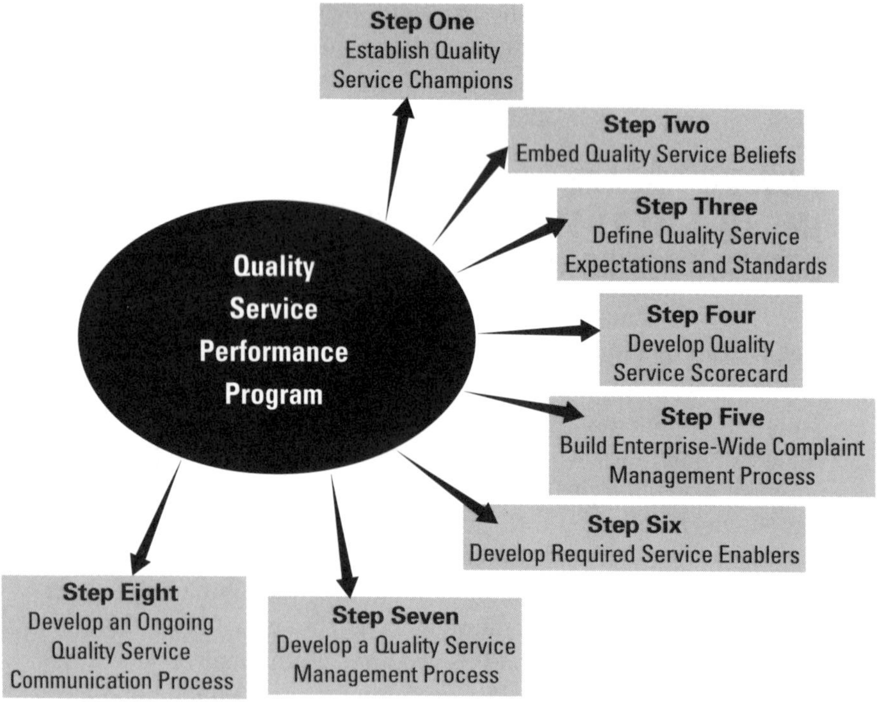

Step One: Establish Quality Service Champions

Identify one or more individuals to create, manage and drive the success of the Quality Service Performance Program. Champions should be appointed by whoever has responsibility over ensuring that the CRM vision is obtained and they are not necessarily at the management level in the organization. Some organizations have allowed each unit in the company to nominate its own champion. The champions' current role in the organization is not as important as having the right skills and attitude (for example, they need to be highly motivated, customer focused, able to motivate others, good communicators and respected in the organization). Having champions to consistently track the success of the program can ensure:

- effective management of the program

- keeping the commitment to continuous improvement alive

- innovation and creativity

- strong and sustained leadership

Make sure that individuals are chosen with the required qualifications (skill set, experience and appropriate responsibility within organization). They must be given the time required to make the commitment. To support these champions, establish a team or council with representatives from each management unit across the organization and include some frontline staff.

Step Two: Embed Quality Service Beliefs

Establish and communicate broadly quality service principals and fundamentals (e.g., service first) to generate awareness, excitement and commitment to quality service throughout the entire organization. Your probability of success increases if each staff member understands his or her value in the initiative. This is often achieved through a mix of good communication initiatives that include broader staff meetings and individual coaching sessions. Consider conducting a series of quality service workshops to get input on the key principals and fundamentals for quality service. Have the employees own this from the very beginning. A real demonstration and commitment to embedding quality service beliefs is to create a Customer Bill of Rights (CBR), which speaks to the level of quality service your customers can expect.

A CBR clearly states what your customers should expect from your organization. It explains to your employees what customer standards you expect them to deliver. The CBR is proudly posted on the wall in full sight of your customers. Regardless of the industry sector, the purpose of a CBR is twofold. One, it tells your employees what's expected of them as a routine standard of performance. Secondly, the CBR publicly makes a bold commitment to your customers concerning how they will be treated and serviced.

The CBR is generally a bottom-up document, with significant input from the customer and frontline staff. It is a document that clearly states what the company is prepared to deliver to the customer (what it wants to be known for) and what it is prepared to be measured against. It is a public document that is unabashedly sent out to customers and, with some companies, posted on the back of all invoices.

Your Customer Bill of Rights should clearly and concisely say what you are prepared to deliver to your customers. The following is a typical CBR example for the hotel business.

Our customers have a right to:

- Get through to reservations without waiting and to receive prompt, courteous service and accurate information in the official language of their choice.

- Receive the best room available at the time of reservation in the price range requested.

- Receive cheerful, efficient and hassle-free service, and be treated with care and compassion from the time they enter the property to the time they depart.

- Enter a clean, comfortable room with basic amenities that include soap, hand lotion, shower cap, and in-room devices such as telephones, mini-bars, televisions and convertors that are in working order and user-friendly.

- Be informed of the availability and cost of all services before use and receive accurate, timely and consistent billing for services used.

- Have confidentiality respected.

- Receive value-for-money in all their food-related experiences.

- Be informed when there are delays or when things go wrong, and be treated with extra care in these circumstances.

- Comment on his/her guest experience, and receive prompt response to comments, concerns and suggestions.

In addition to the CBR, institute a program to communicate service beliefs to all staff on a regular basis. For example, the Ritz Carlton holds five-minute morning meetings each day to communicate and discuss their commitment to quality. The responsibility for setting the agenda and running the meetings rotates with all staff. They are informal "hallway" meetings, but participation is expected by all. The meetings are primarily for short-term gain—they discuss what can be done immediately to improve customer service. Staff recognition is also promoted at these meetings. For example, stories of great customer service by a specific staff person are shared.

Step Three: Define Quality Service Expectations and Standards

Determine how your customers would define optimal quality service, and then define a set of balanced performance measures and appropriate weightings that reflect this definition. Ensure that you measure the right things according to your CRM vision, strategy, objectives, leading practices and how your customers define quality customer service. From this, clearly define service expectations and standards based on the quality service principals and fundamentals established in Step Two. Staff will have a greater success rate if they know exactly what is expected of them. Measuring against established expectations and standards will highlight performance gaps and facilitate continuous improvement.

A number of critical success factors must be in place for this step to have any impact on staff. They are as follows:

- Publish service expectations and standards to all staff, and remind them that this program is motivational and its primary purpose is continuous improvement. Do not keep this a secret—do this through the Customer Bill of Rights or through a mission statement-type of document.

- Encourage staff to participate in developing performance measurements, and solicit input at every stage. Hold performance measurement workshops to help develop measures throughout the organization. Post the initial list of measures on your internal Web site, and ask for input. Hold contests for the best performance measurement list created by staff.

- Promote self-measurement and self-training, even peer coaching. For example, if using an automated quality scorecard, allow access to the scorecard for 15 minutes per day for each staff person to conduct a self-test on himself or herself; the results are never seen by anyone but the individual staff person. Develop a peer coaching program that is fun and offers rewards for superior coaches (employees that are recognized by their peers as such).

- Try to make it fun. Hold contests, offer prizes to most involved staff, use the internal Web site to hold daily quizzes, and implement a series of screen shots that pop up during the day on employees computers that stress quality service expectations and standards.

Step Four: Develop a Quality Service Scorecard

Develop and test a balanced quality service scorecard. A quality service scorecard measures if you are delivering service at the level of quality defined by your customers. The key to developing the scorecard is to first survey your customers for their definition of quality. From this, develop a scorecard that measures all the components of this definition. For example, your customers may define quality service as accurate, friendly, complete and reliable service. The scorecard should measure these components. If speed of service is not important to your customers, your quality service scorecard should not measure this.

Your scorecard helps you understand how you are performing relative to customer expectations. A balanced scorecard will enable standardized and objective measurement to ensure high-quality service to all your customers regardless of location, service or channel. Your scorecard should promote superior performance, enable you to pinpoint staff development and training needs and reduce costs through improved service. Most organizations struggle with how to execute this. The process should provide feedback to correct or reinforce behaviors; this is also an important way to communicate with all employees. A key strategy to motivate and retain staff is to provide feedback that demonstrates the individual's progress in meeting personal career objectives and how personal contributions affect quality service performance throughout the organization. However, many organizations fail to achieve these benefits because of the administrative burdens such processes can create. Most of the administrative burdens are a result of using a manual paper-driven scorecard. Effective objective scorecards require much detail, which lengthens the scorecard (often to about 20 pages). Technology solutions and process tools are available that help to automate the process and eliminate the administrative barriers to implementation.

When developing a quality service scorecard, remember to do the following:

- Measure proactively—don't score down! Don't start with 100 points and take away points (mark down) if the employee falls short of perfection.
- Set targets and stretch targets for staff, but be realistic.
- Create an easy-to-use measurement tool for frontline staff members, which they can use to improve quality.
- Identify precise activities that illustrate the desired behavior. For instance, give samples of outstanding quality service such as an appropriate tone of voice to manage a difficult customer.
- It is important to pilot-test, evaluate and modify a scorecard. However, prior to making changes to the scorecard or finalizing it, conduct focus groups and feedback sessions with both frontline staff and performance evaluators to solicit changes or improvements. The scorecard should remain consistent for a number of years since it should contain the expected level of service and also allow for scoring the exceptional level of service. If you begin to outscore the scorecard, whereby the majority of staff are scoring at the exceptional level, the scorecard was designed too simplistically.

To be successful, the scorecard has to contain enough detail to ensure objectivity, but not so much detail that evaluators and staff get bogged down. It should be very clear and detail what is expected of staff, and an easy and fast way to improve performance must be evident.

Step Five: Build an Enterprise-Wide Complaint Management Process

Develop a systematic easily accessible management process capturing actionable information from both employees and customers on compliments, complaints and concerns about your service. This contributes to the enterprise-wide continuous improvement commitment. To be successful, the process must ensure:

- a fast and efficient issue resolution system
- a fast and efficient best practice identification and sharing process

This process must proactively encourage customers and employees to give feedback—and it is critical to ensure that their suggestions are recognized. The selection of feedback categories within the process must be simple and concise. Don't get bogged down in the detail of categories. Focus on implementing results and acting on customer feedback. Make it easy to provide feedback.

Step Six: Develop Required Service Enablers

Service enablers are activities, policies, processes or tools (e.g., CRM technologies, online manuals, e-training workshops aimed at improving customer service that staff can complete in short time frames such as pop-up quizzes that take 10 minutes to complete) that encourage and succeed at improving quality service specific to organizational and individual needs. Without service enablers, organizations struggle to reach optimal performance. The absence of service enablers makes it almost impossible to improve continuosly. Continuous improvement requires an investment in staff, technology and structure—these are all considered service enablers. Develop the short-term (e.g., a coaching program to deal with demanding customers, telephone scripts, enhanced IVR system) and long-term requirements (full CRM technology). This will help to prioritize where you spend your money.

Step Seven: Develop a Quality Service Management Process

Develop a quality service management process that focuses on managing staff performance and training staff. The objective of this process is to result in a cycle of progressive improvement by delivering the appropriate coaching, training and/or counseling in the right manner (see Part Four, Chapter 10 for more information on this). Your process should have the flexibility to accommodate evolving employee and customer needs, growth and complexities. A quality service management process results in staff wanting to do better and increase their level of quality service. It creates a nonthreatening environment whereby performance gaps are not punitively approached. Staff are comfortable and, in fact, look forward to performance discussions with management since this is viewed by staff as an open, fair and learning process.

Step Eight: Develop an Ongoing Quality Service Communication Process

The most often-cited complaint of staff is either too little or noneffective communication. Ongoing communication about your QSPP will enable a clear understanding of organizational quality service objectives, initiatives and how far you have come. The communication plan should include advising staff of any training plans to support them in their improvement journey. The plan should also outline corporate, management and frontline staff information requirements and how these will be met (e.g., communicated over the Web on a weekly basis or through a newsletter). Although numerous methods of communication channels can exist (Web, paper, meetings, conference calls), it is important to brand and standardize every method of communication (print, meetings, web-casts). Branding (e.g., developing a logo) and standardization demonstrate that this is a long-term organizational commitment and helps to continue to excite staff.

Some organizations have designed shirts, mugs and memo pads with their quality service logo. The logo should also be on all print material and welcome staff as they log onto the web site. Communicating staff success stories and new initiatives aimed at quality service improvements go a long way in encouraging staff to continuously improve and remain dedicated to the commitment to measure quality service and continuously improve. Although there must be a primary responsibility center for all communication, as many staff as possible should be encouraged to communicate customer service success stories. It is also critical to have your champions and senior management communicate progress on a regular basis (e.g., a message from your champions in a monthly newsletter).

IMPROVING QUALITY SERVICE THROUGH THE RIGHT PERFORMANCE PROGRAM

If you have already implemented a Quality Service Performance Program, you may be unaware that you are focused on practices that are *reducing* quality service rather than continuously improving it. Got your attention? If yes, answer the following questions:

- Are you focused stricly on quantitative measure and not spending enough time and attention to the quality (accuracy, tone, customer management) of the customer interaction?

- Do you know what is being said to your customers over the telephone or in person when your customers call in?

- Are your customer service representatives reinforcing your marketing message, or are they sending conflicting messages?

- Are you getting the impact you require with your customers, one of creating loyalty?

- Does your organization encourage your frontline employees to learn from their mistakes and to *continuously improve* their performance through self-measurement and objective scorecards?

If you answered "no" to even one of these questions, then you're not practicing continuous quality service improvement.

These questions are critical, and the answers, as they apply to your organization, may be startling. Fortunately, you are not alone. Many organizations have attempted to improve quality service performance and achieve improved practices through a single-minded focus on quantitative performance measures, with little attention to the qualitative components that drive customer satisfaction and customer loyalty (quality of interaction, accuracy and completeness of information provided). These systems have been too focused on the metrics themselves, often only quantitative metrics (number of customers, length of customer wait time), without due attention to measuring, monitoring and managing outcomes such as increased customer loyalty, and focus on an environment of continuous improvement.

Qualitative measures include measuring the following:

- accuracy and completeness of the information provided

- employees' communication and customer management skills

- how customers are greeted

- how employees complete the service

- how employees handle difficult customers

To be successful, the Quality Service Performance Program must be both quantitative and qualitative and must have at its foundation a scorecard that is built on performance information that does the following:

- Assists the organization in making better, informed decisions around what is required to improve quality service across the organization and with a specific employee.

- Improves allocation of CRM resources by demonstrating where more people, money and time are needed to ensure quality service.

- Invites continuous improvement by advising where improvements can be made and where best in class is being met.

- Promotes and demonstrates CRM accountability throughout the organization at every level with every individual. For example, scorecards are completed at every level of the organization that are linked to one another so that the performance of one level of the organization influences the performance of the next level. Individual employee scorecards are linked to their managers, the manager's scorecards are linked to their superior and so on, right to the president/CEO of the organization.

Sound difficult? Yes, but it is also tremendously beneficial. What follows is a best practice example of success.

A CASE FOR CHANGE— PERFORMANCE DRIVEN CHANGE

We recently had the opportunity to work with a multinational organization in developing its Quality Service Performance Program. The company first developed a process to measure, improve and ensure consistent high-quality telephone performance. The organization had outsourced the delivery of its customer service function to multiple (over 50) independent contractor call centers nationally. Collectively, the call centres were responsible for answering over 15.5 million customer calls annually, with no common performance and quality measures to service these customers.

There was a driving need to perform in a consistent manner across the country, but to start, the need to create a baseline and implement a continuous improvement process for the following fiscal year was the priority.

Actions Taken

Working with the client, we set out to develop and test a set of foundational tools that could ensure consistency and quality improvement. The following tools were developed:

- a standardized scorecard
- a scoring calibration process (the means for qualifying objective versus subjective quality assessments through increasing the impartiality of the quality call monitoring by increasing the consistency of the scoring)
- a sample plan (a schedule that indicates which employee will be monitored at what time of day, day of the week and week of the month)
- management information reports
- third-party monitoring validation process

The scorecard consisted of seven quality performance measures (the greeting, communication skills, CRM skills, protocol skills, accuracy of information, the closing and post service action). Each was supported by a detailed definition of how to score for each point. Each of the seven quality measures had a different weighting depending on its importance to the overall definition of quality, as defined through customer focus groups (e.g., accuracy was weighted more than the closing). To facilitate scoring, tabulating and reporting, an Internet application was created. In addition, as all the call centers were self-reporting, to ensure data integrity, a third-party validation process was instituted. We conducted research with well over a 100 call centers to determine best practices. We were all surprised by our two critical learnings. The first was that although all call centers measured quantitatively, almost none measured quality of service. The second discovery was that our research uncovered a fundamental flaw that went unnoticed in almost all of the QSPPs we reviewed. We found that there was a wrong way and a right way to improve performance.

Improving Telephone Performance— The Wrong Way

Organizations can improve their quality service, employee satisfaction and cost savings by encouraging employees to not only operate at an *expected* quality performance level, but also offer them the opportunity to *exceed* those standards. As research indicates, the majority of quality call monitoring programs measure their employees against the "perfect call" (which would relate to a score of 100 percent or 100 points). If the employee falls short of this perfect standard, the employees get marked down. Organizations that employ this type of performance monitoring unknowingly encourage two things to happen: First, the employees know that no matter how hard they try, it is extremely difficult to perform at a 100 percent level, and it is certainly impossible to exceed that. So why bother trying? Second, the employees begin to feel discouraged by getting marked down, and their performance deteriorates even further. For example, if you are marked *down* to 80 percent, you feel you have lost points and have not performed well. If you are marked up to 80 percent and have the ability to get over 100 percent, you feel encouraged to do better.

> "If you think of standardization as the best that you know today, but which is to be improved tomorrow, you get somewhere."
> —Henry Ford

Improving Telephone Performance— The Right Way

Once organizations make the shift to a quality call monitoring program that promotes continuous improvement, they will intuitively encourage employees to *exceed* expected performance levels. Once employees understand their own level of performance and what actions are required to get to the next level, more often than not, they will try to exceed expectations.

As a result of scoring the right way, organizations will be in a stronger position to retain employees, satisfy their customers and reduce operating costs. By concentrating efforts on *selected* performance measures (e.g., telephone interaction skills, accuracy of information provided etc.) that require improvement, rather than lumping *all* performance criteria together (some of which may not require improvement), organizations can improve the efficiency in their call center operations.

A Quality Service Performance Program, with a commitment to continuous improvement, was developed. A quality service scorecard was designed with its performance measures based on a one to five (one being unacceptable and a five being outstanding) level proficiency scale (see Figure 5-2).

Figure 5–2   Scoring Proficiency Levels

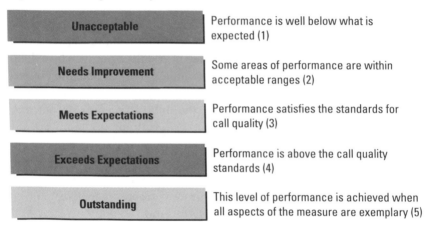

Unacceptable	Performance is well below what is expected (1)
Needs Improvement	Some areas of performance are within acceptable ranges (2)
Meets Expectations	Performance satisfies the standards for call quality (3)
Exceeds Expectations	Performance is above the call quality standards (4)
Outstanding	This level of performance is achieved when all aspects of the measure are exemplary (5)

The organization set an expected performance level at the proficiency level of three; this would meet customer expectations, and employees are considered sound performers. This allowed employees to operate at the expected performance level while encouraging exceptional/leading practices performance through the proficiency levels of four and five. The employees not only knew what level they were required to perform at, but they also knew what had to be done to exceed expectations. However, it was also important to acknowledge to all staff that the expected percentage of employees who scored a four or five was very low. In a group of 50 employees, 30, on average would be performing at a level of three, 15 at a level of a four and only about five would perform at a level of five.

First Round of Results

Only a few months following the program's national implementation (following an eight-week pilot and a national training program), the organization witnessed considerable improvements from their contractors in specified areas of telephone performance. The organization is now confident that contractors are aware of areas that require improvement and are taking action. The tools and techniques that have been developed have laid an important foundation, leading to national standardization of quality service, employee empowerment and continuous improvement.

Importance of the e-Channel

Because of the urgent need to establish a standard for national quality service, the development of the program was put on an accelerated path. The goal was to go live in nine months (develop and implement the program in nine months), which typically would take about 16 months to complete. In our nine months, we focused on building the tools required to measure performance consistently and objectively. We knew that in order to measure consistently and objectively across all 50+ call centers required a high level of detail (e.g., all measures and proficiency scales needed detailed definitions) and that we needed to automate and enable the system into a Web-based full end-to-end tool—one that incorporated quality monitoring, workforce management and training tool (more on these types of tools in Part Three).

The power of a Web-based tool was significant. The speed at which results were available (real-time results with automated analysis of scoring and immediate reporting capabilities built in), the assurance of a consistent approach (using automation allowed for very detailed definitions to be presented on screen) and the reduction for the need to calibrate, coach and train was substantial. All of this translated into significant dollar savings, and even the cost to use and update the scorecard was reduced. But, maybe more importantly, the speed and ease of the Web enabled an improvement in quality service almost immediately upon our "go live" date since staff could see the results of their scores immediately and could improve upon them. In the more traditional process of manually scoring on paper, results are often shared weekly or monthly to allow for analysis to occur.

We built a scorecard that is believed to be differentiated from all the rest. Feedback from call center managers, supervisors, quality monitors and customer service representatives has been positive. Perhaps the most significant result of the Web-enabled tool is the ability to promote measuring performance as a strong, empowering, performance driven CRM application that builds staff and customer loyalty.

Improving your organization's telephone performance by shifting your focus from quantitative to qualitative measures is an undertaking that requires dedication and commitment. Doing it the *right way* will improve your customer satisfaction, but it will also increase employee retention, reduce operating and training costs and bring you closer to becoming a *best in class* organization. Committing to quality service through the development and implementation of a Quality Service Performance Program is critical to your performance driven CRM efforts. Providing quality service drives revenue up. There are eight steps in developing your QSPP, but the most critical element is the development and implementation of a quality scorecard that measures the right way. In the end, customers remember only the actual customer experience. If it was one of high quality, the chances of them abandoning their loyalty is low. If they remember their experience as one of poor customer service, they will abandon your organization and drive revenue down. As Howard W. Newton once said, *"People forget how fast you did a job, but they remember how well you did it."*

Part Three

The Tools to Build and Enable the Performance Programs: Overview

OVERVIEW

Technology and people must go hand in hand. Faster, smarter technologies must be seen as tools to not only equip an organization with faster, smarter customer representatives, but also to provide the ability to measure and manage for continuous improvement. Our research, in part through our syndicated IDEAS[1] research studies over the past 10 years, found that the most common organizational challenges to support performance driven CRM include:

- knowledge management tools
- the need for tools to support continuous improvement
- the need to improve customer contact
- the need to better measure productivity
- the need for new advanced training tools

There's more. However important external customers are to the success of your business, the real key to success may, in fact, be your internal customers, your customer service representatives (CSRs). CSRs are the new front line. To be successful, they require excellent client service skills, strong product knowledge and increased customer knowledge.

Numerous tools are being used by leading organizations to help their employees become effective. They include the following:

- the use of standard benchmark models across the organization to assist in evaluating the strengths and weaknesses of each customer contact
- performance measurement and monitoring tools and technology and incentive programs to provide additional assurance of high customer service levels

---

[1] IDEAS (Innovative approaches to Deliver performance and Excellence through improved practices and Service delivery) is a seris of nine syndicated studies conducted by PwC Consulting since 1991 as a barometer of global customer care practices.

- performance support systems, which combine several technologies, including expert systems that provide advice

- computer-aided instruction to train and educate customers, suppliers and customer support staff

Best practices organizations also take a strategic approach to organizational, customer and quality service performance programs, as you will note in the chapters that follow. How an organization achieves best practices in workforce management is not a quick fix formula that can be picked off the shelf and installed; nor is technology the solution. There are many pieces to this puzzle, and that is why we offer these best practices considerations:

- Keep your CRM vision relevant and alive. The performance information can be used to cycle back to the vision each year to bring it in line to reflect new customer needs.

- Maintain a focus on key areas required to achieve the overall CRM vision. Analyze the performance information, and identify if you are getting closer to the vision.

- Make available information required to align the organization to its CRM vision, available to not only senior management, but to those on the front line. The information can show where shifts in staff or more staff are required.

- Build internal organizational commitment by showing staff the improvements that are made.

- Build and sustain customer loyalty by contributing information that assists in managing customer, business and internal organizational relationships.

- Identify requirements for change levers such as change management workshops, customer service training and new technology solutions.

Chapter 6 provides guidance on enabling the Customer Performance Program. A well-enabled program should be capable of measuring and gaining an understanding of the customers, their habits and their likes and dislikes. But unlike traditional CRM, these measurements must highlight strengths and deficiencies and be used to spark continuous improvement. In traditional CRM, performance information has to be acquired on the following:

- who the customers are and their needs
- customer purchasing patterns
- the impact of marketing and/or communication efforts
- the match between services and products and customer needs
- current levels of customer satisfaction

In performance driven CRM, this gathered information must be compared against required standards, standards necessary to drive lasting CRM. Gaps in performance must be addressed, and corrective action should be taken to achieve continuous improvement.

So what is an organization to do to deal with this monumental challenge? What tools are most appropriate to drive the Customer Performance Program, and which will drive increased knowledge of the customers, their habits and trends? In Chapter 6, we will provide a range of traditional- and technology-charged tools that will take you down this path.

Chapter 7 highlights the tools and technologies to support an Organizational Performance Program (OPP)—tools and technologies to help manage workload, scheduling and training and to ensure that there is organizational alignment and commitment to the components of performance driven CRM. In this part and in the following Part Four, the importance of the contact center and its alignment with other organizational units comes to the forefront. To achieve lasting CRM—performance driven CRM—the contact center and its management must embrace new tools to monitor, measure and manage the service delivery.

In Chapter 7, new proven tools are presented that build upon leading practices across a wide variety of industries, tools that support the critical success factors of committed leadership—fully integrated role alignment.

Chapter 8 closes this section of the book with a description of the required nontechnology-based tools (sometimes referred to as processes) that are required for your Quality Service Performance Program (QSPP), our third and critical performance program to ensure lasting CRM. In order to fully implement a Quality Service Performance Program that is committed to continuous improvement, technology will play a secondary role—it is the enabler, not the driver of change. As discussed earlier, successful performance driven CRM initiatives start with a CRM vision and then ensure that the processes that touch the customer are consistent with that vision. They must be customer-friendly and efficient and be capable of delivering quality service. Once they have been designed and embraced, technology is then selected to enable the processes to achieve performance driven CRM.

Process issues are a critical component of the QSPP. They must be aligned with the Customer Performance Program and Organizational Performance Program. Therefore, as the chapter will address, the following are required:

- a continuous improvement framework built around a comprehensive *Quality Scorecard* that sets expectations and measures and provides the basis for coaching and training

- a positive and proactive method for providing employee feedback on performance—a *Coaching Program* that encourages staff performance improvement and aligns staff behaviors and responsibilities with your CRM vision

- an *Employee Performance Agreement* process/template that supports effective communication of accountabilities, requirements and achievement between the employee and organization

- a self-assessment that captures how well your Quality Service Performance Program is doing and whether you are maximizing the benefits of your program

Chapter 8 deals with the above four tools, providing detailed templates and exercises to let you start immediately. Together, the four tools complete your Quality Service Performance Program, and the three chapters in Part Three provide the roadmap. Read on.

The Tools and Technology Required for Creating the Customer Performance Program

Listening and understanding are integral to the health of any relationship, and the one you have with your customers is no exception. When you observe your customers' interactions with your company, you are listening to their needs and wants, and by doing so, you can understand them better. Armed with this information, you can improve the health of your business.

In developing the Customer Performance Program (CPP), you must measure and gain an understanding of your customers, their habits and their likes and dislikes. On an ongoing basis, performance information has to be acquired on:

- who the customers are and their needs
- customer purchasing patterns
- the impact of marketing and/or communication efforts
- the match between services and products and customer needs
- current levels of customer satisfaction

This information must then be used to:

- plot current customer needs, wants and expectations

- predict where customer needs, wants and expectations are growing

- predict future customer needs, wants and expectations

And you are going to need help in collecting, analyzing and using the information. That is the objective of this chapter.

Firms feel pressure to build CRM solutions for many reasons: competition, customer complaints or the pursuit of profits. But poor organizational readiness and a chaotic market create the potential to drive costs skyward. Forrester, a research institute, searched Dow Jones's content base of more than 6,000 business publications for references to CRM; there were only 442 articles in 1998 but a whopping 6,048 in 2000. The pressure on global firms to get their CRM acts together grows for the following reasons:

- Standard-setters inspire—With apps that turbocharge cross-selling or proactively report failures, pioneers such as Capital One and Compaq prove that CRM pays.

- Tales of poor service proliferate—The recent *BusinessWeek* cover article, "Why Service Stinks," epitomizes the drumbeat of deteriorating service[1]. Even marquee firms such as Amazon.com and AT&T struggle to balance aided and self-service. Reflecting the trend, the University of Michigan Business School's American Customer Satisfaction Index (a yearly survey on the level of customer satisfaction across the United States) declined an average of 7.9 percent between 1994 and 2000. Service has deteriorated, and the facts, in this case, do not lie.

- Firms scramble to find profitable customers and cut service costs— As the softening US economy ratchets up attention to the bottom line, firms consistently report that cost-cutting is their primary or secondary goal[2]. Yet the Net's promise to cut service costs and boost profits remains elusive, as 41 percent of online customers prefer the phone as their primary channel, resisting self-service alternatives. Is it that the Web is not providing the right level of detail, is it a basic view that this channel is not secure or is it just that customers do not find this channel customer-friendly?

So what is an organization to do to deal with this monumental challenge? Which tools are most appropriate to drive the Customer

---

[1] *Business Week*, October 23, 2000.

[2] November 1999, Forrester Report "Driving Sales With Service."

Performance Program, and which will drive increased knowledge of the customer, their habits and trends. In the sections that follow, we will provide a range of traditional and CRM-related tools that will take you down this path. Traditional tools include:

- Quantitative Research
- Mystery Shopper Surveys
- Personal Interviews

CRM-related tools include:

- Segmentation and Data Mining/Modeling
- Customer Management Systems
- Customer Relationship Portals

What are you doing, and how far down the path have you gone?

TRADITIONAL TOOLS

Most organizations use the traditional tools of market and customer research as part of their performance driven CRM initiative. Most CRM initiatives will utilize one or more of these tools when initially setting up their CRM vision. But as we highlighted earlier in this book, to achieve performance driven CRM, one must initially start with measures/standards and benchmarks, and following that, a mechanism to measure, monitor and create change—change in process, actions, organizational structure and people competencies are required. CRM can survive only with continuous performance improvement.

In Chapter 3, we highlighted the "where" and "what" that had to be measured. What follows is the "how." For most organizations, this is not a core competency, nor a suggested one. For that reason, to ensure objectivity and be in a position to utilize the latest in survey techniques and analysis, most organizations use external resources to administer these survey options.

Confused about what to use and when? Here's a guide for the traditional tools, which include: quantitative research, mystery shopper surveys and personal interviews:

Quantitative Research

This form of research, which is traditionally done through telephone contact, is primarily used to collect "hard numbers" or representative data on the entire customer base (ratings on all aspects of quality service, direct comments and opinions on the service experience). It can also be used on an ongoing basis for tracking or monitoring purposes and as input to a CSI (Customer Satisfaction Index).

Mystery Shopper Surveys

This is a tool used to test service levels. A trained individual will observe the service practices of an organization and then report in a standard report format.

While not directly a method to gain an understanding of the customer, it is a means of looking through the eyes of the customer and to assist in defining all the contact points, service features and problems associated with each. It provides verification of problem points, and can be used as part of an incentive or appraisal program for service personnel. It is used primarily for a large customer base, low relationships and many or few transactions. Typically, after the performance driven CRM initiative is put in place, this tool will be used to gauge, in a more qualitative manner, the success of the implementation and enable more rapid change. The results are often used as a basis of individualized training. Although it was originally developed in the retail sector, it is now widely used in all sectors.

This tool is used to collect information on a specific service experience and is generally used to supplement market research surveys by providing information from selected individuals on a few key areas. This tool provides an opportunity for direct feedback to the service provider and for ensuring that quality standards are continuously maintained.

Personal Interviews

Personal, one-on-one interviews are used primarily with high-value customers and to monitor the quality of service provided through personal observation. It is too expensive, and perhaps not cost justifiable, to do personal interviews with all customers, but it is essential that your most valuable, strategic customers are given special treatment. Again, it is advisable to use third parties to conduct these interviews since objectivity and skilled probing is required. Customer discontent or dissatisfaction with product features or even staff members will usually come to the forefront more willingly in these types of customer interventions.

This tool, while possibly the most effective in allowing the organization to uncover deeply rooted issues, is quite expensive to administer, and thus, it is used primarily with the most strategic customers.

There are several other methods of conducting personal interviews. These include:

- Team Visits
- Customer Panels
- Toll-Free Telephone Line
- Warranty/Registration/Comment Cards
- Customer Service Department/Customer Call Centre
- Conventions and Trade Shows

Team Visits

These are personal visits at the customer site, using cross-functional members of an organization—sales, purchasing, distribution—to observe how the customer is using the product and other issues that might arise. This technique is generally used to provide insight into how the customer uses the product/service and the problems or unmet needs that may exist. It also allows employees to develop value-added solutions designed specifically for each customer. Most organizations use this for situations that cover a small customer base where a strong close relationship with the customer is desirable.

Customer Panels

This entails a carefully selected group of customers invited on a regularly defined schedule to comment on new product, service or strategy enhancements. This provides an opportunity to communicate on an ongoing basis with key customers, experts, etc. Customers see value in this since they now feel that their opinions are valued and that they can now have a greater impact on issues that affect them. There is usually no remuneration for participation, and, as such, it is a relatively inexpensive means of obtaining feedback on changing needs and reactions to newly initiated improvements (especially high-tech).

Toll-Free Telephone Line

This is a 1-800 number customers can use to contact their supplier to report on customer service issues. This method is useful in obtaining many types of information from customers as a supplement to market research as well as providing information to customers. It represents a point of entry into what may be perceived as a "faceless" organization and is used for a large customer base, low relationship and many or few transactions situations. In an effort to be a business that is easy to do business with, organizations are facilitating the means by which customers can provide input and be closer to the organization. As this channel does not require a live agent at the end of the line, this service is available 24 hours a day, seven days a week.

Warranty/Registration/Comment Cards

These are mailed surveys that have a brief set of questions, mailed shortly after the purchase of a product or after a recent service call. An often-overlooked tool, this technique assists in providing timely information on the most recent contact with the organization. Rather than a phone survey months after the last interaction with the organization, this mail-out captures information shortly after the last contact. It can also be used to obtain demographics and shopping habits of the customers. Some organizations also use this as a further supplement to market research, and as a means of tracking customer problems and complaints, and perceived product strengths.

Customer Service Department/ Customer Call Center

This is a key point of contact with the customer and a critical opportunity to "get close to customers" and to win their loyalty. Comments and interactions with the customer, while not generally willingly solicited, are an important source of information on problems and unmet needs. In some organizations, questions are posed to the customer just prior to the completion of the call. In other cases, customer complaints or issues are logged into a complaint management software tool for tracking and further analysis. Future opportunities to improve performance and increase customer satisfaction can also be identified.

Conventions and Trade Shows

This technique is held by your organization or industry—and maybe even your competition. It is a useful means of communicating with "hard to reach" customers (e.g., doctors, scientists and certain other professionals). By attracting these individuals to your booth, through demos, draws or product information booklets and then interacting with these professionals, it will allow you to obtain direct information on current satisfaction levels, service enhancements, competitive offerings, unmet needs etc. (and may be combined with a quantitative on-site survey). This means of interacting with the customer is most suitable for a large customer base, high or low relationship and low transaction situations.

A Guide for How and Why to Measure Customer Issues

Performance driven CRM requires an organization to set standards, measure against those standards, and then use that information for continuous improvement. At times, this information can be used for the creation of a new vision or strategic direction, product enhancements, organizational realignment or prioritization of issues that will require more immediate action. What follows is a guide on what issues can be addressed through a more vigorous approach to customer interaction, together with the most effective tools that will facilitate that data collection and what is provided. The issues include:

- Strategic Direction
- Creative Focus
- Implementation
- Reaction to Market Feedback

Strategic Direction

Tools: Historical data, market situation analysis, external experts, future scenario research, secondary research

Provides: Higher level customer understanding that identifies basic market needs and shapes the strategies for broad-scale technology and business investments

Creative Focus

Tools: Customer panels, customer visits, market research, trade shows, sales calls

Provides: Processed customer information that is the basis for creatively defining new product and service concepts

Implementation

Tools: Customer panels and site visits, test markets (trade trials), market research, quality function deployment, customer feedback

Provides: Processed customer information that represents the stated customer requirements for product performance, features and benefits that drive product definition activities

Reaction to Market Feedback

Tools: Customer feedback, Sales education and customer interface, customer satisfaction studies including lost sale studies, customer visits, sales calls

Provides: Processed information that results from customer responses to products, services and marketing activities

There are many examples that demonstrate the effectiveness of using the tools described above, but the example of the organization that follows, Honeywell, in creating and using its Customer Performance Program, sheds light on the importance of this step in the process of achieving performance driven CRM with its strategic customers.

CASE STUDY
Honeywell—Integrated Customer Relationship Management Strategies[3]

While an organization should be praised for soliciting customer feedback, if the organization does not have the ability to respond in a timely manner, more harm than goodwill will be created. As well, if the organization is unable to use that customer feedback for continuous improvement and changes in operating practice to enhance customer satisfaction and loyalty, it will not achieve lasting CRM. Such was the case with Honeywell and the impetus behind the creation of its integrated, performance driven customer relationship management initiative.

Honeywell's Pacific division did not have a Customer Performance Program; rather, its original approach was focused on customer satisfaction, similar to that of many other companies. Its annual customer satisfaction survey was conducted with customers over the telephone by a third-party research firm. The survey consisted of closed- and open-ended questions, with results tracked from year to year and then provided to the senior management team.

But there were limitations to this annual survey methodology, including:

• long feedback cycle

• anonymous customer data

• information given to directors first, frontline last

• poor overall response rate

Honeywell took action to improve its process with the following primary objectives in mind:

• obtain customer feedback

• gain ability to respond to customer concerns

• institute changes necessary to improve organizational performance

---

[3] Strategic Account Management Association, *Velocity Magazine*, Vol. 2, No. 2, 2nd Quarter, 2000.

- enhance customer satisfaction and customer loyalty
- benchmark internally and externally

This led to the birth of its Customer Performance Program and the tool to enable it—the real-time survey process.

Real-Time Surveys: Conceptual Design

Honeywell developed its first version of the real-time survey in 1996 to measure and track customer satisfaction over the life of an installation project. The survey could be completed with a customer on the telephone within five to seven minutes. Customers were also asked to state how often they were willing to be surveyed: monthly, bimonthly or quarterly.

With the survey, a process to propel performance driven CRM, which encompassed new standards and measures, organizational realignment and a new approach to quality service—led to continuous improvement. To conduct the surveys, Honeywell created an internal survey business unit called the Customer Advocate. This unit was responsible for not only the survey tool, but the dissemination of information leading to continuous improvement. The survey has since been revised and now consists of seven attributes plus overall satisfaction and a "likelihood to recommend" question. "Likelihood to recommend" is used as the key performance indicator (KPI), in particular, the percentage of customers that rate a 4 (quite likely) or a 5 (very likely) to recommend Honeywell to others. (The actual survey tool is not available as this is deemed proprietary.)

Real-Time Survey—The Process

The first step toward implementing real-time surveys was to register customers to participate in the process. A one-page kick-off sheet was used by Honeywell customer contacts to introduce and explain the survey process. The kick-off sheet asked customers to rate the importance of the seven attributes that would be used in the survey. These attributes could relate to the degree of satisfaction with the following:

- sales force
- degree of marketing support
- order process

- after-sales service

- value for money

- strategic alignment with the customer

Customers also had the opportunity to add additional attributes of particular importance. These importance scores were used as a comparison against the actual performance ratings customers provide on a continual basis—that is, are the areas that are of highest importance to customers the areas in which the organization does well or poorly?

Conducting surveys with customers is really only the beginning of the Customer Performance Program (CPP). Communicating the results to the appropriate customer team is the next step. Putting the data into the hands of the employees who impact customer satisfaction directly is powerful; however it must be done carefully to ensure that customer relationships are enhanced. To that end, a training course—Customer Relationship Management, Phase 1—was developed with the help of the Customer Advocate. One of the most important parts of the course was the introduction of a "closing the loop" model with customers within a week to 10 days after a survey had been conducted.

Now, here is where performance driven CRM kicks in. Survey results are used as input for performance effectiveness reviews, and outstanding results and favorable customer comments are used as a key determinant for employee reward and recognition. Specific customer comments are communicated to the appropriate departments for follow-up and action (e.g., product managers and software developers and account executives). And directors receive monthly reports that include all customer comments and team action plans.

Benefits

After one year of using the real-time methodology, an internal survey was conducted with employees to determine their satisfaction with the real-time survey process versus annual customer surveys. The real-time survey process is clearly preferred by Honeywell employees: 83 percent rated the real-time survey process a 4 or 5 on a five-point scale (where 5 is the highest score) for the ability of the

CPP to highlight action items, as opposed to 22 percent for the previous annual surveys. Similar results were reported in areas such as timeliness of receiving information, ability to understand the information, usefulness of results and visibility in the company.

The results that really matter, however, are the improvements in customers willingness to recommend Honeywell to others. Customers show a 20 percent increase in their willingness to recommend Honeywell over the base year prior to the initiation of the CPP.

The tool to enable it, the real-time survey process, empowers employees to take responsibility for their own customers' satisfaction. It also meets the criteria of an effective customer satisfaction measurement program, allowing tracking and trending and statistical analysis. The primary focus, however, remains on creating a performance driven CRM culture that places a high value on customer feedback and finding new, creative ways to meet customer needs.

CRM-RELATED TOOLS

Traditional customer satisfaction tools alone cannot provide sufficient information to propel performance driven CRM. An effective Customer Performance Program requires a number of CRM-related measurement tools to provide timely and strategic information: segmentation and data mining/modeling, customer management systems and customer relationship portals. We discuss each in turn.

Segmentation and Data Mining/Modeling

Recognizing that some customers are more important than others, a strong segmentation methodology is required, and once obtained, information on the strategic customers must be collected, analyzed and synthesized. Thus, the need exists for effective data extraction tools (to reshape and analyze the data). To be effective, it is important to start with a strong foundation and built on an ability to recognize those customers that will have the greatest impact on your success. But dividing customers into groups and gathering information sporadically will not drive an enhanced ability to create lasting CRM. Below, we start with the traditional principles of segmentation, and the new measurement and management requirements to drive continuous improvement.

These include: customer segmentation, sales segmentation, and data mining/modeling.

Customer Segmentation

There are many variations on the theme of segmentation. The more traditional methods start with breaking down your customer base into recognizable and manageable groups. By profiling your customers and dividing them into segments, you can target those groups more specifically to their needs. Additionally, you can measure actual behavior of those groups over time against expected results. Segmentation can be done using cluster analysis (demographic, psychographic and behavioral characteristics) and should be done at least once a year or whenever significant changes are made in your company's business model. Try to avoid demographic-only segments, and build segments based on behavioral characteristics. These will better define who your customers really are.

One of the newly popularized variations is based on customer value. This concept is gaining in popularity as a key tool for segmentation. To achieve this segmentation, organizations must evaluate the market and individual customers based on each customer's overall value. Business decisions are not based on just how much total revenue a customer provides. Rather, decisions are based on total customer value to the organization. A company should determine customer value by looking at both quantitative and qualitative data, such as the following:

- What is the customer's potential growth?
- Is the customer price conscious or someone who is looking for value-added enhanced services?
- How much does the account cost to provide service?

With that information in hand, a company can measure the variable cost of each customer and then prioritize. It can then determine the top 10, 20 and 30 percent of customers. That information can then be shared with every employee by a special symbol, which appears next to top customers' names. Customers with high potential can be highlighted with a different symbol and are treated as potential top-ranking customers for a period of time.

The next step, however, is to set standards and measures against each of these segments, the—Customer Performance Program (CPP). Then monitor against those to identify when or if any corrective action must be taken, by customer segment, to drive enhanced customer satisfaction, loyalty or increased sales attention.

Sales Segmentation

Within the CPP, it must be recognized that different customer segments require different sales attention and sales focus. Thus, the need exists for sales segmentation and the management and measurement of sales resources against the various segments. This form of segmentation involves dividing customers and prospects into categories in order to use sales time more efficiently. The group of customers that promises the most profit and the prospects that have the most dedicated sales time allotted to them—the A group—get the most face time with the salesperson, including personal phone calls and visits. The companies in the B group are not as promising, but they have some potential and so get phone calls and letters but less one-on-one attention. The C group, composed of customers and prospects with the least potential, receive even less attention.

Segmentation may sound like an obvious idea, but companies usually do not change their sales practices until something, such as a slower economy, forces a change. These companies have to focus their sales efforts on the more profitable prospects. Driven by the need for greater efficiency, time management and prospect management software programs are used to assist in that process. These software programs, which are sometimes described as Contact Management or CRM suite software, offer an ability to track time dedicated to a customer, sales history, prospects and leads, callbacks and follow-up required, as well as a number of other useful tracking and time management functions.

According to Jeff Tanner, director of research at the Center for Professional Selling at Baylor University, a typical salesperson spends only one-third of work time actually in front of prospects. The rest of the time is spent on paperwork, such as filling out purchase orders, recording contacts and preparing activity reports.

With time management software, however, a salesperson can document activities in the computer and download information to the sales manager, leaving more time to actually sell products. Sales jobs will become more "sales pure" by using technology to handle the administrative side of sales. As members of the sales force learn to embrace the technology, they will become even more productive.

Data Mining/Modeling

Data mining helps you understand who your customers are by how they behave. With this information, companies are able to create models to target certain customer segments with marketing promotions to drive revenue and build market share.

As part of the larger process known as knowledge discovery, data mining is the process of extracting information from large volumes of data. This is achieved by grouping data, looking for trends within this grouped or segmented data, looking for common behavior or buying patterns and then displaying it in a manner that will lead to more effective campaigns or improved customer satisfaction.

Why Use Data Mining?

In today's fast-paced and competitive business environment, it is becoming increasingly harder for businesses to maintain their competitive advantage. Every day, companies process and store vast amounts of highly detailed information about customers, markets, products and processes. By mining this data, organizations are able to resolve a diverse range of business problems and create new opportunities.

What Can Data Mining Do?

Data mining is a process that allows computers to look for patterns in information. By digging deep into the transactional records of prior experiences, companies can anticipate future consumer behavior and look for trends. It's a building block tool, necessary for uncovering the demographics of customers. Data mining techniques can be used to achieve a wide range of goals within different industries. Here are some of the things they have been used to do:

- Identify profitable customers and their characteristics.
- Predict customer buying behavior.
- Rank customer defection for effective retention programs.
- Focus marketing efforts on prospects more likely to purchase.
- Evaluate advertising effectiveness.
- Evaluate and prioritize credit risk.
- Estimate potential customer seriousness.
- Cross-sell and upsell customers based on past product purchases.

- Target direct marketing to those most likely to respond.

- Predict fraud.

- Optimize share of wallet.

Data Mining Models

Here are six of the more popular and effective data mining models used in order to gain an understanding of the customer and maintain a Customer Performance Program[4]:

1. Retention and Attrition Modeling

2. Risk Avoidance Modeling

3. Cross-sell Modeling

4. Profitability Modeling

5. Click Analysis Modeling

6. Predictive Modeling

We discuss each in turn.

1. Retention and Attrition Modeling: Retaining your highest-value customers and knowing which ones are at risk of leaving can dramatically impact your profitability.

- Do you know which of your customers are defecting to the competition and why?

- Do you know which of your high-value customers are at risk?

- Are you spending your retention dollars on your highest-value customers?

- Do you have meaningful and cost effective ways to contact your customers on a frequent basis?

It is inevitable that businesses lose customers. Through an analysis of the data, models can be built to predict the likelihood of customers departing, or being attracted to certain sales promotions or campaigns. With these models, you can determine those customers with the highest propensity to cut back or discontinue business by profiling those who have left in the past. A retention model examines the potential for a customer to be retained after some event. An attrition model considers the

---

[4] Extracted, in part, from the AARM Relationship Marketing Report, a publication of the Association for the Advancement of Relationship Marketing.

likelihood that an active customer will stop buying from you. With this information, proactive goals can be set and customers can be actively pursued or flagged for special attention.

2. Risk Avoidance Modeling: How can you avoid acquiring unprofitable customers? Data mining can predict, with some accuracy, which prospects will become customers. However, it is also particularly helpful to determine which customers will be profitable. It is also important to recognize that some new customers will default and force your company to write off losses. Therefore, risk management and marketing groups must work together when new business programs are put in place. While marketing is looking for increased revenue, risk management examines the new business that could turn out to be unprofitable. Both disciplines should work together to evaluate the marketing efforts that are based on the insights gathered. Look to your risk management group members to see how they can participate proactively in your next marketing campaign. Use models that are built to identify profiles of new customers who will default (another type of likelihood model) and existing customers who will turn bad. These models examine purchase behavior, payment behavior, credit profiles and other factors.

3. Cross-Sell Modeling: Cross-selling and upselling are central to successful CRM. Interacting with your customers is a prime opportunity to market additional products or services. What have your customers been buying? What are their interests? What products or services have they been looking at or inquiring about? We can look at the data in different ways. First, what products or services have the best cross-sell potential judging from past sales data? In other words, which products have been purchased by a single customer most often? Next, what are the customer profiles that best match various product groups? When you identify customers who have a tendency to purchase like products but you haven't approached them yet, you have an excellent opportunity to promote that product to your existing customers. That's what CRM is all about. We've seen Amazon.com do this very well. When you visit your personalized site, you'll see the message, "Welcome, here are books and CDs that might interest you." This can be accomplished by modeling product purchases by individuals over time and grouping them.

This example, although used before in the book *Customer Relationship Management*[5] provides a good example of cross-sell modeling.

---

[5] *Customer Relationship Management; A Strategic Imperative in the World of e-Business,* Stanley A. Brown, Toronto: John Wiley and Sons Canada, 2000.

CASE STUDY
Capital One

Capital One Financial Corp. ranks in the top 10 largest issuers of credit cards in the United States. In 1997, Capital One realized the emergence of serious dissatisfaction with its level of customer service. The company's customers were expressing their discontent with the time it took to have their issues handled by customer service.

Capital One realized that it would lose its customers fast if it couldn't get them to the right place at the right time. Thus spawned the organization's information-based strategy, which combined information technology (data warehousing) and analysis (data mining) that helped the company to identify, manage and execute new ways of doing business. Capital One began to analyze customer calling patterns to determine why customers would pick up the phone and make a call. New technology (Intelligent call routing) was implemented. This essentially predicted why the call was being made and who would be the best agent to service the request. High-speed computers, which gather background information on US households and typical Capital One customer behavior, took just milliseconds to identify who was calling and why, pick the best person to notify and forward essential information about the person calling. In turn, information was also acquired as to what this customer would be likely to buy (once the original issue had been resolved) even though that would be far from the nature of the customer's call.

As a result of the data warehousing and data mining efforts, questions could be answered before they are even asked, calls last a third of the time that they used to, customers are satisfied and the cost of the call is reduced. In addition, through much research and numerous tests, as is now part of Capital One's culture, the company discovered that customers were more likely to purchase something if they called you for something else as opposed to traditional outbound telemarketing. Therefore, while customers were already on the phone and satisfied with the response to their request, a Capital One agent, armed with information from the company's data warehouse, would offer them another opportunity. The opportunity would be to purchase a product ranging from auto insurance, mortgages, long-distance service, auto loans etc.—special offers to preferred Capital One customers. The added advantage of the new implemented technology became that the route customers' calls took had as much to do with why they were calling as to what the organization knew they would be interested in buying. In 1998, half of all Capital One's new customers bought another product from the company within a year of signing up for their credit cards.

4. Profitability Modeling: How can you measure and affect the lifetime value (LTV) of your customers? What will they buy, or potentially buy, over the course of their purchase lifetime? Any basic data mining analytics package will include ways of calculating LTV and using it to segment customers. Even recency-frequency-monetary (RFM) models—how recently have they purchased, and how frequently might they buy—which are founding members of customer analytics, will contribute greatly toward understanding your customers so that you may communicate with them more effectively. Understanding the key components of profitability will help you understand when and if your customers will become profitable.

5. Click Analysis Modeling: Clicking behavior, or how a customer navigates through the pages on your Web site, can be captured and analyzed to understand customer behavior and preferences. How long they spend on a page, which links are clicked on, which ads get the most hits, where the person enters and exits the site etc. all become statistical information for that company's database. The data become useful because now companies know what sells, how to position the products and what other ancillary items may be of interest to their customers. If a lot of time is spent clicking through outdoor grills, chances are this user may be in the market for grilling tools as well. It also shows page abandonment rate—what pages are skipped, avoided or cause the viewer to leave the site—indicating the pages that need further evaluation for content and ease of use.

Click analysis software (there are a number of commercially available ones) is robust; however, on its own, it fails to give a complete picture of each visitor at the site. It would be hard to ascertain if visitors are buying products for themselves or as gifts, if the customers are profitable or browsers etc. The demographics of the target market cannot be established using click analysis tools alone.

6. Predictive Modeling: This is a very proactive approach to understanding your customers. Mathematical and behavioral sciences are applied to predict better how, when and why a customer will purchase from you. In great demand today, these technologies can begin to predict what other products, services and information you can offer to your customers that will benefit each one. Additionally, it can predict when customers are about to leave (attrition)—who and why—and establish corrective actions to keep those relationships that you've worked so diligently to establish.

By utilizing multiple types of technologies (e.g., click analysis, data mining and predictive modeling), a company moves beyond the concept of selling to servicing its customers. Companies that understand their clients' value chains will be the ones to bank on in the future.

Customer Management Systems

Your most strategic customers will warrant differentiated treatment. Thus, customer management tools are necessary to manage the customer experience, to direct customers to the most optimal channels and track the effectiveness of these channels in delivering customer satisfaction, loyalty and retention.

Customer management systems, sometimes referred to as CRM systems or suites, are now available for enterprises of all sizes. These software systems allow the organization to track and maintain customer history, issues and complaints and manage opportunities and the sales cycle and customer preferences by channel. Implementing this technology enhances a business's ability to attract and retain customers; but it is equally critical that these systems be used as input to a Customer Performance Program (CPP). Here's how they can be used.

There are very few areas remaining in which a company can differentiate itself from its competition. In fact, most enterprises have automated their sales forces to some extent, if only to equip them with handheld or laptop computers running a contact manager. Chris Fletcher, an analyst with the Aberdeen Group, estimates that 85 to 90 percent of all salespeople use some kind of technology to assist with sales. But, he also states that fewer than 25 percent of Fortune 500 companies have implemented true customer management tools.

For those companies looking to jump ahead of the pack, customer management can lead the way. Here's how it works. Employees are better able to do their jobs, an ability that translates into increased satisfaction, lower turnover, and a higher quality of work. Customers are satisfied, sometimes even impressed, with the company's attention to detail. And satisfied customers are much more likely to return for repeat business, which will pay dividends many times over.

Once a customer management system is in place and your business starts to reap the rewards, the amount of information in the system increases, further facilitating its use. And the more information the system contains, the easier it is to justify the investment in software, infrastructure, training and implementation. Next to tying a customer management solution in with sales, the marketing and service departments are the most obvious points of contact you should connect. Because the Internet is such a prominent presence today, savvy marketing is one way of spreading the net wide to gather in multitudes of potential customers.

If you don't link marketing to your overall customer management solution, you leave open the proverbial barn door. When visitors to a business's Web site qualify themselves as potential customers by requesting information, filling out a survey, or perhaps entering a contest, a business can capture that information and route it to the proper product champion for a quick response. Capturing information from the corporate Web site is important, as is responding professionally. If the system passes along current and accurate information to other points of contact, follow-up should be fast and professional. To achieve this kind of response may require passing a virtual baton to the telemarketing department to make a follow-up phone call. With marketing and telemarketing linked, there's a greater chance that follow-up will occur. When it does, the telemarketing person will have accurate information on both the customer and the products that the company is selling.

The Contact Center and Customer Experience Management

The integration of the customer contact centre into day-to-day organizational operations represents one of the key emerging trends in the twenty-first century economy. The impact is such that contact centers are expected to affect almost all aspects of society from the private sector to public sector in all parts of the world.

Multimedia, multichannel customer contact centers are at the heart of this changing relationship and are key enablers for companies looking to meet this new challenge. Customers want to contact companies at their convenience, using the most convenient means. Good service is now a survival issue, and the battle is being fought over the perceived value that customers receive from their relationship with their suppliers, and thus, a major focus on the service being delivered by the customer service representative (CSR).

Any contact center dedicated to contributing to the bottom line monitors CSR performance. However, once calls are monitored, what is done with those interactions determines where the real advancements occur. The fast-emerging customer experience management (CEM) strategy and business platform enable contact centers to achieve more with their recorded multimedia interactions by integrating and leveraging the growing list of tools and applications, so that they can close the loop on quality and deliver superior customer services. These include: analytic tools for the contact center; recordings integrated with CRM and eCRM tools; and Web-based survey tools. We discuss each below.

Analytical Tools for the Contact Center

New data mining and data analysis applications are enabling contact centers to transform their wealth of customer interaction data into powerful, actionable knowledge. Until now, call recording and data analysis were completely separate functions. With newer software solutions, data analysis can be fully integrated with call monitoring and recording to provide contact centers with a comprehensive analytical tool that goes far beyond what was previously possible.

By taking information from the automated call distributor (ACD)—the software that routes calls to the appropriate customer service representative and combines it with recordings of those interactions—managers can obtain an end-to-end view of a customer's experience from the time he or she entered the contact center, to the time the call was finished. Managers can get answers to questions such as: "Why are customers placed on hold?" "Why did call volume double between 1:00 and 2:00 p.m.?" "What were these calls about?" "What are the causes of excessively long calls?" At a highly practical level, managers can quickly identify, drill down and play back the calls, which may elicit a new question: "Why are callers to the Campaign X transferred twice, at which point most gave up and hung up?"

Recordings Integrated with CRM and e-CRM Tools

Integrating recording applications with the wide array of available CRM and e-CRM programs enables managers to target specific agents, customers and campaigns. Value-added benefits can be as simple as customizing customer communication by capturing specific caller data, or they can be much more sophisticated. Integration between screen capture (that which is displayed on the customer service representatives computer screen) and e-mail, for instance, allows a manager to search for specific e-mail messages, track the back-and-forth between customer and agent and assess how the agent puts together the e-mail responses. This is a powerful, integrated tool and represents just one example of the potential that exists in contact centers today by integrating recordings with software solutions.

Web-Based Survey Tools

Until recently, a company's understanding of the customer experience was limited to its contact center supervisor or quality group's view of operations. New Web-based survey technologies represent the next step in CRM. Survey tools can import data from your CRM applications to create tailored surveys for different customer segments. It then automatically sends an e-mail invitation to customers to click on a link to a Web survey. In so doing, companies can augment their internal perceptions with direct customer feedback. These customer surveys can then be compared with internal evaluations. One major ISP (Internet Service Provider) surveys 40,000 customers a month, comparing internal evaluations with its customers' opinions to arrive at an internal and external perspective of its contact center.

Customer Relationship Portals

Obviously, information must be accessible by those who need to use it. Thus, the need exists for a customer relationship portal to bring together all the disparate interaction pieces necessary to gain and retain customers.

For many organizations, the goal is to make it easy for customers to do business with the company, let customers help themselves when it's convenient, or receive personalized one-to-one service when they want it. This can be achieved by making sure everything relating to customer contact comes together seamlessly, breaking through technological and organizational barriers. Bringing a customer relationship portal into the contact center is what can make this possible.

Creating strong customer relationships and maintaining them is essential to a company's success. With increased competition, companies are reevaluating their CRM strategies and how their customer contact centers are performing. Customers not only have more choices for how to contact a company but, with 24-hour access to companies all around the world, they have more choice as to which companies they deal with.

Portal software creates a single virtual place at which all customers can meet the enterprise. In addition, a customer relationship portal allows businesses to define business rules easily for customer contacts, allowing businesses to react quickly to the dynamic e-business environment. The portal connects customers with the best resource, whether it's via the company's 800 number, e-mail or Web site. With a customer relationship portal, all the different types of contacts are blended into a common queue. And if a customer sends an e-mail and then calls, the agent knows this because every transaction is retained, routed and utilized with the customer relationship portal.

In addition to consolidating customer contact mediums, a portal in the customer contact center brings together information that is key to a successful CRM strategy—customer data, product information and account information. A customer relationship portal connects to customer databases for easy customer identification and qualification. The portal sits in front of front-office applications to present specific information at the agent desktop. It also pulls information from back-office systems, such as ERP (enterprise resource planning) systems, accounts payable and inventory. Front- and back-office applications hold important information about customers, but their information is often kept in their own separate databases. A portal allows the information that is stored in one to be shared with another. As described earlier in our Capital One and Amazon.com examples, putting the power of complete information at agents' fingertips allows them to be more responsive and proactive with customers.

A customer relationship portal provides consistent information about the customer interaction so businesses can monitor operational efficiency of contact resources and analyze interactions to ensure the business is meeting service objectives. It can provide the means to access marketing and service programs for outcomes and effectiveness.

The customer relationship portal brings together the necessary technology and information, which allows companies to deliver consistent, high-quality service to customers no matter how they choose to contact the enterprise, thus keeping those customers coming back.

SUMMARY

In Chapter 3, we brought out the need for the Customer Performance Program (CPP) and the importance of setting goals and standards against which you must be prepared to be measured. That conceptual framework is the heart and soul of performance driven CRM. But in order to execute against that, one needs to embrace a number of tools and methodologies as key enablers. This chapter provided you with traditional and CRM-related tools. Traditional tools included: quantitative research, mystery shopper surveys and personal interviews. CRM-related tools encompassed: segmentation and data mining/modeling, customer management systems and customer relationship portals.

The importance of data sources can never be underestimated in any data mining or database marketing project. Of course, the most valuable source of information within these type of projects is prior customer behavior. But one interesting challenge concerning data sources is the use of market research data. Traditionally, market research has been used to understand the underlying attitudes and psychographics of consumers comprising broad target audiences. With this information, marketers have been able to refine their communication and message to their audience but within a mass marketing framework.

Whatever your path, remember to set your goals first and then look for the tools to do the job. One of your first goals should be to know your customers and discover whether they are (or aren't) who you thought they were. Listening and paying attention to your customers is critical to any business relationship. Use these tools to listen to your customers and then reach out to them.

But what are you doing and using today? In the following checklist check off those tools that you have embraced or are considering. Leading organizations have incorporated the following in their CRM strategies:

CHECKLIST—CPP TOOLS

Which of the following do you use to build, maintain and apply a single view of a customer?

❏ You are aggressively integrating customer data. Building and maintaining accurate, integrated customer databases allows you to integrate them and recognize customers in real time.

❏ You are bringing together customer records captured from different internal systems. This ensures that customer data gathered through one customer contact point is integrated with other customer touch points and with internal client processes such as sales and marketing.

❏ You are supplementing internally collected information with externally collected demographic information to gain optimal customer intelligence.

❏ You are applying this customer intelligence to real-time customer interaction.

❏ You are strengthening customer data integration expertise and methodologies. The challenges associated with managing huge volumes of customer data across disparate repositories is now amplified by the need for rapid, real-time customer data integration. You need to integrate and analyze customer data within an increasingly shorter period of time.

❏ You are quantifying return on investment (ROI) and developing ongoing measurement processes. In difficult economic times, most organizations are heavily focused on their ROI on previous CRM investments as well as on making a business case for future CRM investments. Quantifying the value that an investment brings is the premise of ROI.

❏ You are recognizing opportunities for integration. Integrating enterprise-wide systems will remain an important opportunity for many organizations. Moving beyond the enterprise, there exist many possibilities in integrating systems with the extended enterprise as well as with the extended enterprise community that includes partners and suppliers.

The Tools and Technology Required for Creating the Organizational Performance Program

As Jim Zetwick, business systems director for Enabling Services, Borden Foods Corporation said, "Imagine a basketball game where nobody on the floor knows the score except the referees—until some point after the game is over, when the winner is announced." That is what your organization is like if you do have not performance information available to your employees. How will they know if they are winning the game or if they have to try harder or change strategies? They can do little about their performance if they get this information too late, after losing the game!

Your Organizational Performance Program (OPP), one of the three critical performance programs required for performance driven CRM (PD CRM), should be designed to improve performance across the organization, resulting in better customer service. However, if you do not have the proper tools and technology to optimize your efforts, you may be fruitless in your efforts.

Performance data from your OPP should be available to anyone at any time. Year-end performance reports are outdated and not valuable. You may have already lost a majority of your customer base by this time. Lagging sales, dropping revenues, increased customer complaints or worse, no customer contact, would have already triggered a sign of trouble. But where would you begin to implement change and improvement without up-to-date organizational performance data?

But before you can use the performance data from your OPP, you must assess where you are in your program development. Chapter 4 described how to build your OPP, but it is important to also be able to understand how far you have come in building your program, how mature (in functionality and implementation) your OPP is. Leading organizations have gone through a maturation process in building their OPP. They move from the first stage in which they are just beginning the OPP, to the final mature stage, the optimal OPP, in which performance driven CRM is being practiced through a highly functional and fully implemented OPP. This stage is reached when customer centricity is entrenched into the organizational culture with the support of appropriate tools and technology. The ability to improve the organization and CRM continuously are the outcomes of this stage.

Achieving optimal OPP requires the organization to progress through the four stages. Figure 7-1 illustrates these four stages. As an organization evolves, it moves from a nonstructured/committed, non-technical environment to a highly structured/committed, technical environment.

Figure 7–1 Four Stages of the Organizational Performance Program

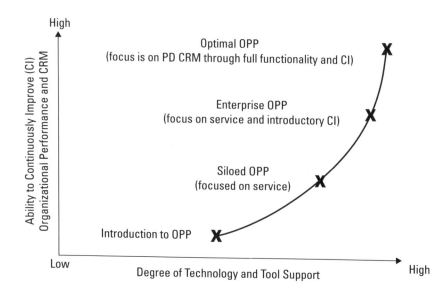

The stages start with the introductory stage, in which simple technology has been acquired and implemented. Hence, the OPP is in its infancy stage. As you build your program, you should advance through each of the stages. However, with careful planning and management of your efforts, it is possible to move from the first stage to the last stage and bypass the second and third stages altogether.

Organizations that have developed their OPP framework, the dimensions, feasible performance measures and indicators with well-defined attributes, baseline and targets have also defined their reporting requirements, are taking action using performance data and are practicing performance driven CRM. These organizations usually have reached the optimal OPP stage. This can be done only through implementation of technology and dedicated people who are skilled at developing performance measures. Most organizations have yet to reach the optimal OPP stage. Many are at the siloed OPP stage, in which organizational performance is being measured and performance data is being used to make positive changes, but this is being done in a siloed fashion—e.g., within individual units with various technologies, not across the organization.

THE OPP DIAGNOSTIC

To determine where you are, your organization must assess itself against a series of critical success factors. Use the OPP diagnostic at the end of this chapter to help you determine what stage you are currently at. The OPP diagnostic can also be a tool to help you determine what you have to do to move into the next stage.

The optimal OPP stage is achieved by ensuring that all of the critical success factors are fully realized and maintained. At times, an organization may have evolved into a more mature stage but may find that as a result of rapid business growth, major technology implementation hurdles, significant changes to service delivery or shifts in organizational structure, it has moved backward. It is important to self-diagnose occasionally, even if you have achieved the final mature stage.

ACHIEVING THE OPTIMAL OPP STAGE

There are nine organizational requirements to achieving the optimal OPP stage:

1. Committed Leadership
2. Full Integration
3. Role Alignment
4. Defined Customers
5. Anchored Accountability
6. Clear Documentation
7. Dynamic Reporting
8. Continuous Improvement
9. Embedded Process

Committed Leadership

Leading organizations define this requirement as having staff members in the organization who are champions of the OPP—who are fully engaged in the program and act as leaders in terms of demonstrating commitment and support for the OPP. They ensure that any blockages are unblocked and that momentum for the program continues. Committed leadership also includes developing a customer-focused motto, based on performance results, that drives customer-centric behavior.

Full Integration

Leading organizations define this requirement as having all of their organizations' business management processes (business/strategic planning, budget allocations) integrated with the program. The program is fully integrated with the customer segmentation strategy through technology. For example, organizational performance is organized by customer group and service levels. The CRM strategy incorporates the program as a means to operationalize targeted value propositions, and all HR processes (compensation, hiring, training) are linked to the program.

Role Alignment

Leading organizations define this requirement as having all employees understand that what they do matters to performance driven CRM.

Communication by senior management to all levels of the organization occurs at appropriate/effective intervals.

Defined Customers

Leading organizations define this requirement as having both the Customer Performance Program (CPP) and the Quality Service Performance Programs (QSPP) integrated with the OPP. The concept of "one customer" is embedded into the culture. For example, the same customer profiles are available to all business units, and customers are serviced consistently regardless of where they enter the organization.

Anchored Accountability

Leading organizations define this requirement as having a high degree of trust and accountability in the organization, a commitment that accepts no excuses for nonperformance, a consistent reliability in meeting minimum performance standards across the organization and stretch targets that are being realized by those that have the ability.

Clear Documentation

Leading organizations believe that having a documentation process is not necessarily required as the program becomes second nature. Documentation clearly demonstrates that qualitative measures begin to outweigh the importance of quantitative measures.

Dynamic Reporting

Leading organizations define this requirement as having accurate, timely, appropriately detailed reporting combined with the use of supporting technology and color coding for performance management ease (e.g., poor performance is highlighted in red, good performance is highlighted in green and performance that is moving toward being poor is highlighted in yellow). In addition, reporting is visually appealing has the capability of multiple reporting levels of various detail and is able to forecast resource needs and to trend past performance. Intranet performance reporting capability is realized, and the organization is maximizing the use of Internet tools.

Continuous Improvement

Leading organizations define this requirement as having continuous improvement as part of the day-to-day analysis and activities.

Embedded Process

Leading organizations define this requirement as having no real reliance on documented terminology because the program definitions are so well known that they have become second nature. When a customer-centric view is inculcated into the culture with the objective being customer loyalty, the process is embedded.

Below, we examine the case of Sears and how the company has implemented some of the nine requirements to achieve optimal OPP. While our goal is to highlight the OPP, included you will find threads of CPP and QSPP. The message is that quite obviously, an effective performance driven CRM initiative needs all three components.

CASE STUDY

Sears Roebuck & Company

Sears Roebuck & Company is a leading household goods retailer with approximately 330,000 employees in 2,900 locations across North America. In 1992, amid increasing competition, primarily from Wal-Mart, Sears suffered a US$3 billion loss. This competitive shock triggered a major downsizing, restructuring and replacements at the most senior levels of the organization.

The new executive team shaped a vision for Sears based on performance in each of what have become known as the "three compellings," making Sears a compelling place to shop, work and invest. All activity undertaken by employees at every level was aligned to one or more of these three compellings. The implementation of this vision has helped propel Sears back to profitability, culminating in a record US$2.4 billion in operating earnings for 1999.

Sears's attributes its success to its simple vision, which was based on total performance indicators (TPI), an ubiquitous and simple communication message, tied directly to vision and a variable pay system tied to the TPI. At the heart of this are ongoing customer and employee satisfaction surveys and detailed statistical analysis. But the company does not stop there. It has created a simple, user-friendly intranet site for sharing of good practices across departments and locations and a unique training and orientation tool, which is based on learning maps that plot the customer experience and changes in customer needs over time.

Strategy for Embedding Vision Deep into the Organization

This corporate vision of the "three compellings" has embedded itself so deeply into the organization that the terminology of the vision is commonly understood and quoted by employees at all levels. The basic strategy for enabling this level of infusion was by simplifying the vision so it could be communicated through an easily recognizable message. The simple three compellings icon is everywhere: on computer screensavers, employees' service pins, corporate clothing, training materials, award certificates and anywhere elsewhere appropriate. Sears executives understand that when they consider the vision established and even passé, it is only just filtering down to ground-level staff. Management is therefore committed to refreshing the image and meaning every two to three years. Executives keep the vision alive among their own ranks by tying variable pay to performance in each of the three compellings. Originally, the variable pay breakdown was financially focused: 25 percent work, 25 percent shop, and 50 percent invest. However, based on the improved understanding of what drives financial performance, the percentages have been revised to 33 percent each.

Executives need to achieve threshold targets to receive stock payouts; otherwise, they receive options. Further, a chairman's award is presented to staff who embody all three elements of the vision.

Customer Satisfaction (CS) and Employee Satisfaction (ES) Measurement

Two surveys are used to gauge customer satisfaction and one to gauge employee satisfaction:

External Shopper Survey (ESS)

This is a "blind" tracking study in which purchasers rate Sears and other competitors on a variety of attributes including shopping experience by category and imagery in stores.

Pure Selling Environment (PSE)

This is an IVR (interactive voice response) survey focusing on loyalty and total satisfaction for Sears shoppers. To encourage shoppers to call the IVR and partake in the survey, Sears offers customers a $5 discount on their next shopping trip, which results in an excellent 30 percent response rate.

My Opinion Counts Employee Survey

This is a survey completed annually by all employees in which they are asked to rate their experience of working in the Sears organization.

In order to define the correct "drivers" of customer or employee satisfaction, Sears conducts significant amounts of statistical research. There is an understanding that drivers are different from "outcomes" and that it is critical to identify the right drivers to get meaningful results in terms of likely outcomes. For example, using factor and cluster analysis, Sears translates its 18 customer satisfaction categories into four drivers—people, place, product and value—and three outcomes—reputation, satisfaction and loyalty. The original categories are based on research from employees, customers and other external research. It is not expected that the categories will be perfect, and changes are made if the reason is compelling.

Customer Satisfaction and Employee Satisfaction Data Analysis and Linkages

For the main customer satisfaction survey (PSE), the rating scale was recently increased from four to 10 points. This was made to increase the visibility of differences. For example, the key reported metric of satisfaction was shifted from average overall satisfaction score to percent 10. This is the percentage of customers that rated Sears a perfect 10 out of 10. This change was instituted because Sears's research determined that there was a very significant increase in the loyalty rating of "likelihood" to "definitely shop again" between customers who rated overall satisfaction as 10 versus 9. This implies that to achieve true loyalty, it is necessary to achieve perfect satisfaction scores.

The most significant discovery about the links between ES, CS and profitability is that there is a causal link between financial performance and customer satisfaction scores. As well, there is a significant relationship between employees' attitudes about their job and company, staff turnover and company financial performance. Through statistical manipulation of its model, Sears is able to pinpoint discrete actions—such as improve training or ensure fair treatment by management—that have the greatest impact on revenue.

Success Sharing—Process and Technology

Sears has developed a simple, user-focused knowledge intranet with best practices, survey results, customer comments, tutorials and store rankings. The site is easily navigated and searchable on a wide variety of parameters. There are a number of value-added features, such as "store matching." This allows stores of a particular profile to compare their performance and learn from other stores that are similar to them. To encourage use of the site, rewards (certificates, shirts etc.) are provided to staff members who submit practices, whose practices are selected for entry into the site and who read the site.

PERFORMANCE PROGRAM SCORECARD

Start using technology early on in the development of your organizational scorecard. This will facilitate the management of the performance measures and indicators and will promote early successes in scorecard implementation. There are many types of off-the-shelf performance measurement and performance-based scorecard software available. There are also Web-based scorecard software programs. The major difference is in their capacity to display performance data in a variety of unique views. A performance view is the way data is presented to the reader: it can be by performance measure, by geographical area, by sales, by successful target achievement etc.

Costs for this type of software are various, but the return on investment is possibly quite high depending on how fully you utilize it. However, many organizations fail to maximize the return on investment because they fail to utilize fully all of the capabilities of the software. Some would say the software is only as useful as the data is accurate. Others, who have realized full return on investment, would say that the software is only as good as the organizational commitment to using performance data to drive CRM decisions (including staffing, product, budget, process decisions). You can load the software, but if you don't use the information you can get out of it to make progressive (and, at times, substantial) changes, then your OPP will stagnate and become a costly, ineffective venture.

The decision about which software to buy should be made on the basis of the requirements of your program and your own personal preferences. However, regardless of which software package you chose, in order to be successful at your OPP, the software must:

- Be easy to use and easy to manage. If it is too complicated, only a few individuals will use it, and an enterprise program will never be achieved.

- Assist in streamlining your OPP, not add complexity and confusion.

- Be able to visually compare planned versus actual performance.

- Have a data import facility. Conversion of current data is a must.

- Have the ability to custom defined user security and authority levels. This means that the administrator is able to grant permission to users to plan, track, input data and/or view performance in various parts of the organization.

- Be able to assign performance owners to enhance accountability in the program.

The ability to report performance is critical to your program. Look for solutions that address the following specific reporting functions:

- It reports on the achievement of strategic objectives in addition to reporting on performance measures.
- It provides the capacity to have both detailed and summarized reports. Featuring a variety of graphs and charts of performance results.
- It provides an analysis by objective. This means that you should be able to view complete performance by objective. All measures related to that objective should be able to be viewed on one screen in order to determine cause and effect of one measure on another (e.g., see how advertising expenditures have impacted sales over the past 12 months).
- It has a "trends" feature that provides reporting and graphing over several periods (e.g., year over year, month over month, past five years etc.)
- It has reporting performance gap assessments for each performance measure. This assessment should allow for a narrative section to cover what is happening, why it is happening, which corrective actions are being taken and the expected impact of these actions.

In addition, when selecting your software solution, look for:

- a solution that is quick and easy to deploy, leading to a faster return on investment
- the ability to be accessed either over the Internet or a corporate intranet site leading to a very economical and efficient solution
- prebuilt queries, reports and analyses and executive dashboards that are all customizable but rich enough to use immediately

If your research leads you to a couple of options choose the one that allows for any expanded functionality such as the inclusion of a complete measurement dictionary (in which all definitions of prepopulated measures are listed) and a "what if" capability.

CONTACT CENTER TECHNOLOGY FOR THE ORGANIZATIONAL PERFORMANCE PROGRAM

The world of contact centers is growing rapidly. Contact centers are starting to occupy the majority of how CRM is implemented and customers are served. Organizations are spending more money on expanding their contact centers and moving the majority of service functionality to them. More and more organizations are either moving service delivery to the contact centers or finding new ways to deliver the services already provided by their contact center. Simply defined, contact centers are facilities that house multiple service delivery channels and provide efficient, effective and usually nonstop service (24/7). Provision of service through the Web, e-mail, fax, phone and inperson are common channels in a contact center.

Because the OPP is a primary factor in performance driven CRM and contact centers are a primary factor in the OPP, measuring the performance of the contact center is critical (as one dimension of the OPP). Further, each of the channels must be measured for the ability to deliver to customer expectations at a minimum cost. This includes measuring the effectiveness of staff delivery service, the effectiveness of management scheduling and the effectiveness of the service delivery channel (e.g., speed of the Internet).

There are many technologies that a mature contact center would require. However, there are a few key technologies that are required to ensure that management is positioned to delivery quality performance. The overall performance will be measured, analyzed and reported by the same software solution chosen for your Organizational Performance Program scorecard. However, quality call monitoring tools, call taping tools and workforce management tools are fundamentals required to achieve high performance.

Quality Call Monitoring Tools

A web-based quality call monitoring tool, pdchange.com measures, analyzes, reports and trains. As this tool is discussed in detail in Chapter 8, we will not repeat that discussion here.

Call Taping Tools

These tools are basically voice loggers that record and store calls for playback. Newer software has expanded capacity into the call monitoring realm and encompasses screen capture and evaluation tools that let you gauge an agent's skill level. Some even include the use of online coaching and training tools that enable you to provide online instruction to agents about skills that need improvement. Most of the tools that are available allow you to record calls and capture screens at random intervals or on demand. A sample plan can then be developed, allowing you to evaluate an agent's performance within a scheduled time frame and for a specific number of recordings. The tools should let you set the times you want and record based on schedules from your workforce management.

Recent enhancements allow you to read agents' e-mail correspondences and view calls/screens in progress so that supervisors can push performance coaching notes to a whiteboard through agents' Web browsers and provide analysis and reports on what agents say during their interactions with customers.

The most enhanced capacity that is now on the market is the ability to monitor the stress levels of agents. This is accomplished by using an algorithm that detects stress levels in agents' and customers' voices. Measuring the stress levels allows intervention when things are not going well between agents and customers (e.g., stress management training).

Workforce Management

Workforce management tools allow for incoming calls to be automatically gated to appropriately skilled frontline workers by linking the forecasting/scheduling and caller history databases. It ensures that you have the right number of people answering calls at the right time to meet service or revenue goals at minimum cost. More enhanced tools allow for scheduling based on agent proficiency, not only skill (proficiency is defined as how quickly an agent handles calls.) When scheduling, the engine takes into account each agent's proficiency rating, as defined by the organization (for example, is each agent skilled/knowledgeable to deal with difficult customers), and ensures that enough agents are staffed, even when there are a number of inexperienced (or less proficient) agents scheduled.

Your tools should also allow for:

- staff attrition to be factored into the planning cycle for long-term forecasting so that just-in-time recruitment occurs
- integrated resource planning and call center management across all sites
- workload to be forecast for 12-18 months in the future and easily adjusted quarterly, monthly and weekly if required
- tracking of forecasting accuracy on a weekly, monthly and yearly basis
- selecting your own business rules (e.g., how you want to schedule and report your information)
- integrating an increasing number of technology solutions smoothly

In choosing your tools, look for the following characteristics:

- ease-of-use-to be able to get up and running quickly and avoid a long implementation cycle
- multiple reports for various levels of the organization
- flexibility to schedule from your single or multiple call centers
- "what if" functionality to explore various customer service scenarios and models
- the ability to identify hiring/cross-training needs and analyze budget/capacity impacts
- ability to schedule employees from different organizations in one or more time zones to create "virtual" contact centers dedicated to a single view of the customer
- automatically schedule regular and nonregular events (week to week, day to day etc.)

In addition to quality call monitoring, call taping and workforce management tools, you should also explore tools that provide the following:

- frontline workers to have online capability to pass on difficult issues/problems to management and receive online direct responses from management to these issues

- an electronic suggestion box
- online suggestion systems to facilitate the submission of employee ideas—the capacity to notify employees as to who is evaluating their ideas and receive weekly feedback as to the status of their ideas
- frontline workers with timely and easy access to pertinent information, including information on customers, products and services, new policies and legislation and anticipated peak calling periods
- online just-in-time training
- desktop information services that include databases to retrieve information and access online procedures manuals

SUMMARY

Once again, the need for information is critical. Performance data from your Organizational Performance Program (OPP) will guide your organization and, as such, must be available to anyone at any time. But to achieve optimal OPP, the organization needs to progress through the four stages. As an organization evolves, it moves from a nonstructured/committed, nontechnical environment, to a highly structured/committed, technical environment—a desirable end state. As you build your program, you should advance through each of the stages.

Organizations that have developed their OPP framework, the dimensions, feasible performance measures and indicators with well-defined attributes, baseline and targets have also defined their reporting requirements, are taking action using performance data and are practicing performance driven CRM. These organizations have usually reached the optimal OPP stage.

There are nine requirements if your OPP is to reach its optimal stage.

1. Committed Leadership
2. Full Integration
3. Role Alignment
4. Defined Customers
5. Anchored Accountability
6. Clear Documentation

7. Dynamic Reporting

8. Continuous Improvement

9. Embedded Process

To determine where your OPP is currently, what you have to do to move up the stages, from the introduction to OPP stage through to the optimal OPP, fill in the diagnostic on the following pages. Once you have establish where you are today, look to the details in the next stage to understand how you would look if you were in a more developed stage.

Table 7.1

Organizational Performance Program Diagnostic—Where Is Your Organization?

Critical Component	Introduction to OPP Stage	Siloed OPP Stage	Enterprise OPP Stage	Optimal OPP Stage
	Your organization is in this stage of the Organizational Performance Program if your process is:	This stage has been reached when your Organizational Performance Program has:	This stage has been reached when your Organizational Performance Program has:	This best in class stage has been reached when your Organizational Performance Program has:
Committed Leadership	☐ Not supported and championed	☐ Designated leaders	☐ Enthusiastic and actively engaged staff	☐ Leaders that are fully engaged ☐ A customer-focused motto based on performance results that drive customer-centric behavior exists
Full Integration	☐ A "one off" activity ☐ Not integrated with the CRM vision	☐ Been designated as a possible feed and support into CRM strategies	☐ A direct feed into all the business management processes ☐ Compensation programs linked to the program	☐ All business management processes (business/strategic planning, budget allocations) integrated with the program ☐ The program is fully integrated to the customer segmentation strategy through technology—meaning organizational performance is measured by customer group and service levels ☐ CRM strategy incorporated (integrated) with the program as a means to operationalize targeted value propositions ☐ All HR processes (compensation, hiring, training) linked to the program

Table 7.1   **Organizational Performance Program Diagnostic—Where Is Your Organization?**

Critical Component	Introduction to OPP Stage	Siloed OPP Stage	Enterprise OPP Stage	Optimal OPP Stage
	Your organization is in this stage of the Organizational Performance Program if your process is:	This stage has been reached when your Organization Performance Program has:	This stage has been reached when your Organizational Performance Program has:	This best in class stage has been reached when your Organizational Performance Program has:
Role Alignment	❑ Not known to staff	❑ A profile in the organization, but communication is inconsistent and not well understood	❑ Staff understanding their role in the program and PD CRM	❑ Staff understanding what they do matters to PD CRM ❑ Communication by senior management to all levels of the organization occurs at appropriate/effective intervals
Defined Customers	❑ Not linked to the Customer Performance Program	❑ Linkages to the Customer Performance Program	❑ Multiple linkages to the Customer Performance Program ❑ Introduced concept of integrated customer feedback into the OPP	❑ Both the Customer and Quality Service Performance Programs integrated with the OPP ❑ The concept of "one customer" embedded into the culture—meaning that all organizational activities revolve around this view

Table 7.1 cont.

Organizational Performance Program Diagnostic—Where Is Your Organization?

Critical Component	Introduction to OPP Stage	Siloed OPP Stage	Enterprise OPP Stage	Optimal OPP Stage
	Your organization is in this stage of the Organizational Performance Program if your process is:	This stage has been reached when your Organization Performance Program has:	This stage has been reached when your Organizational Performance Program has:	This best in class stage has been reached when your Organizational Performance Program has:
Anchored Accountability	❏ Not tied to individuals— no requirements for follow-up or any reporting activity	❏ Clear responsibilities and accountabilities ❏ Remedial activities for nonperformance ❏ An escalation process for critical issues ❏ Peformance tied to compensation	❏ An operating principle that "no excuses for nonperformance are are considered valid" ❏ Reliability in meeting minimum performance standards across the organization	❏ A high degree of trust and accountability in the organization ❏ A commitment that no excuses for nonperformance are considered valid ❏ Consistent reliability in meeting minimum performance standards across the organization ❏ Stretch targets being realized by those that have the ability
Clear Documentation	❏ Not tied to quality service definitions ❏ Represented by basic quantitative measures only	❏ Performance standards and quality definitions defined ❏ Well-defined quantitative measures that are tracked and reported on	❏ Well-defined and detailed performance and quality definitions ❏ Well-defined quantitative measures that are tracked, reported on and followed up on ❏ Basic qualitative measures	❏ Documented process not necessarily being required as the program has become "a way of life" ❏ Qualitative measures outweighing the importance of quantitative measures

Table 7.1 cont.

Organizational Performance Program Diagnostic—Where Is Your Organization?

Critical Component	Introduction to OPP Stage	Siloed OPP Stage	Enterprise OPP Stage	Optimal OPP Stage
	Your organization is in this stage of the Organizational Performance Program if your process is:	This stage has been reached when your Organization Performance Program has:	This stage has been reached when your Organizational Performance Program has:	This best in class stage has been reached when your Organizational Performance Program has:
Dynamic Reporting	❑ Manual reporting only ❑ Not timely ❑ Accuracy and integrity of performance data in question	❑ Accurate, timely, appropriately detailed reporting	❑ Accurate, timely, appropriately detailed reporting combined with use of supporting advanced technology and color coding for performance management ease ❑ The ability to forecast resource needs and to trend past performance	❑ Accurate, timely, appropriately detailed reporting combined with the use of supporting technology and color coding for performance management ease ❑ Reporting that is visually appealing ❑ The capability of multiple reporting levels of various detail ❑ The ability to forecast resource needs and to trend past performance ❑ Intranet performance reporting capability ❑ Maximized use of Internet tools

Table 7.1 cont.

Organizational Performance Program Diagnostic—Where Is Your Organization?

Critical Component	Introduction to OPP Stage	Siloed OPP Stage	Enterprise OPP Stage	Optimal OPP Stage
	Your organization is in this stage of the Organizational Performance Program if your process is:	This stage has been reached when your Organization Performance Program has:	This stage has been reached when your Organizational Performance Program has:	This best in class stage has been reached when your Organizational Performance Program has:
Continuous Improvement	☐ Concept not known in organization	☐ A focus on managing performance data to improve service	☐ Performance data managed in a routine structure process of continuous improvement	☐ Continuous improvement as part of the day-to-day analysis and activities
Embedded Process	☐ Lacking in structure and discipline	☐ The program structure and processes documented	☐ Begun to decrease in the number of documented details required for input and output measures as outcomes become increasingly important ☐ Introduced the concept of "enterprise CRM" with a view that there is only one customer to serve	☐ Terminology no longer being important (so well known, it is second nature) ☐ A customer-centric view inculcated into the culture with the objective being customer loyalty
	☐ No technology/tools	☐ Basic technology/tools	☐ Critical technology/tools	☐ Fully integrated technology/tools

The Tools and Technology Required for Creating the Quality Service Performance Program

Supporting tools and technology are needed to implement a Quality Service Per formance Program (QSPP). The primary method for achieving and continuously improving quality service is through a well-developed and comprehensive quality monitoring program. There are a number of tools and technologies to support an Organizational Performance Program (OPP) and to help manage workload, scheduling and training, but there are very few that will fully assist with the QSPP.

Technologies exist to support or enable quality monitoring and improvement (for example, call taping equipment to monitor calls), but few technology enablers exist to actually complete the quality monitoring. Having said this, there are a number of tools (sometimes referred to as processes) that are required for your Quality Service Performance Program. In order to fully implement a QSPP that is committed to continuous improvement, you will require the following three tools:

1. Continuous Improvement Framework and Quality Scorecard—The framework, which is built around the scorecard, sets expectations and measures and provides the basis for coaching and training.

2. Coaching and Employee Performance Agreements—The coaching program encourages staff performance improvement and aligns

staff behaviors and responsibilities with your CRM vision. It must be a positive and proactive method for providing employee feedback on performance. An employee performance agreement process/template supports effective communication of accountabilities, requirements and achievement between the employee and organization.

3. Self-Assessment Tool—This tool captures how well your QSPP is doing and whether you are maximizing the benefits of your program.

This chapter deals with the above three tools, which together, complete your QSPP.

CONTINUOUS IMPROVEMENT FRAMEWORK AND QUALITY SCORECARD

Continuous Improvement Framework

A continuous improvement framework describes the process that will be used from beginning (the vision) to end (confirming/changing the vision) based on performance data. The framework should be a cycle that loops back to the starting point and keeps working itself around its cycle. The framework should describe the quality vision, what and how quality will be monitored, what will be done with the performance analysis and how action will be taken. The framework allows the organization to understand the entire continuous improvement process and what will happen next in each step of the process. Figure 8-1 demonstrates a sample continuous improvement framework. This sample supports a contact center's Quality Service Performance Program. Although the sample was developed for a contact center, it can easily be adapted to any organization since the concepts contained in the framework are the standard concepts all continuous improvement frameworks should contain.

Figure 8–1   Quality Call Monitoring Continuous Improvement Framework

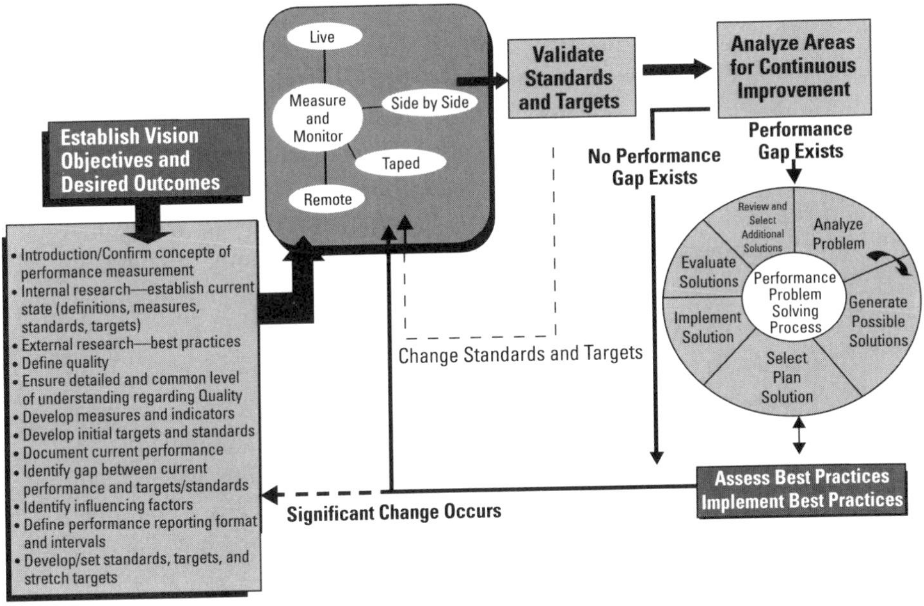

Quality Scorecard

Many scorecards are simple paper-based ones that are used to log performance and do little else. The data from these must be manually inputted into spreadsheets or other tools in order to allow performance to be measured. Many scorecards are limited in nature, so they do not lend themselves to being used as training or new employee assessment tools. For example such a scorecard is one page in length and does not give detailed definitions on how to score staff (e.g., no definitions and/or details are provided for *when* to score poor, fair or good). Once the scores are completed on paper, to get an overall score, a spreadsheet with manual inputs is required.

There are a number of characteristics a best in class quality scorecard contains. The scorecard should not simply measure quality of service. It must go beyond that and be proactive in promoting measurement in a positive manner (for example, allow staff to be marked as exceptional, thereby motivating staff to do better and be monitored). This is accomplished by ensuring that the scorecard is viewed as a "carrot rather than a stick." This means that staff are not penalized for poor performance; rather, they are encouraged to move up the scale. Previous performance is used as a benchmark against which to measures future improvements. Furthermore, a scorecard developed to support continuous improvement must do the following:

- Be specific and descriptive in the standards that are required for quality service. In addition, the scorecard should be specific about what is unacceptable, what needs improvement, what is good, what is very good and what is exceptional performance. This will not only support measurement of current performance, but will provide enough detail to the employee for future improvement or training.

- Assist with reducing the need for routine, broad-based training by acting as a training tool itself and also pinpointing where an individual requires training, where a specific team requires training and/or where training is required enterprise-wide.

- Be all encompassing. The scorecard should focus on improving performance around how customers are managed and the accuracy and completeness of information. Combining these areas into one scorecard will result in a reduction in the time it takes to service customers. It will also reduce callbacks and return visits for the same service and/or complaints.

- Increase employee satisfaction and morale, thereby reducing costs associated with labor turnover such as employee recruiting and training.

- Be available to all staff in the organization. The scorecard should be available to staff conducting the monitoring and those who are being monitored. The tool should be easily accessible, reliable and consistent, and it should take advantage of modern technology (e.g., be Web-based rather than paper-based).

There are not very many off-the-shelf quality scorecards on the market. Those that are available are very customizable. In fact, most can be referred to as a "blank sheet," whereby the organization is required to define quality and the associated areas to be measured by the scorecard. Although there is a degree of comfort in the fact that you get to customize the scorecard to your specific needs, it also means that you have to have the necessary skill and resources to "build" the tool. Self-built scorecards are also very susceptible to individual judgment and definition of what is quality.

The following is a sample of a PwC Consulting Web-based quality scorecard that focuses on the quality of service at a contact center. Specifically, the scorecard measures, analyzes and reports on the call quality. Although this example is specific to call quality, the design concepts are applicable to all quality scorecards.

pdchange.com— A PwC Consulting Web-Based Quality Scorecard

pdchange.com is a Web-based quality service scorecard that is designed to improve performance and customer service by assessing and analyzing quality call performance within contact centers. Although it is first and foremost a monitoring tool, it is also used to coach employees to excellence. This scorecard was developed using leading industry practices. For example, over 100 scorecards were reviewed, and focus groups with staff, customers and management were completed to understand their definition of a great scorecard. The vision was to enable contact centers to evaluate and improve customer service quickly and effectively, while ultimately increasing productivity and morale, reducing expenditures and increasing revenue.

The pdchange scorecard does this by providing a fair, objective quality measurement, analysis and coaching tool that encourages performance enhancement by indicating, in easy-to-follow detail the following:

- areas in which employees need to improve

- what the individual employee needs to do to make the improvement

- how much they have improved by highlighting when they have improved and when exceptional performance occurs

Once the performance data is captured in pdchange, the information should be used to:

• Coach employees to excellence.

• Reduce the need for overall training by acting as a self-training tool for employees.

• Demonstrate in which areas training is most required by individual, team, contact center.

• Improve performance around call handling, accuracy and completeness of information.

• Reduce length of calls, callbacks, and complaints.

• Increase staff retention by improving morale and employee satisfaction. When staff members improve their level of quality service, they feel better about their jobs. When they feel better about their jobs, they provide better customer service. When they provide better customer service, their morale and employee satisfaction increases.

In addition, pdchange creates parameters that make individual definitions of quality consistent and standardized across the organization regardless of how many contact centers there are or their geographical distribution by containing detailed definitions on scoring criteria. This limits subjectivity, and all staff members feel they are being measured the same way. Staff react positively to scorecards that have an increased possibility of an objective, unbiased and impartial evaluation of quality. This means that each performance reviewer scores as close as possible, and in the same manner, as another performance reviewer, regardless of his or her location.

What Should Your Scorecard Measure?

Your scorecard should be based on quality measures that are supported by detailed performance indicators and proficiency levels. Each quality measure should be rated against proficiency levels that are based on a five-point scale. But most importantly, the definition of quality against which the scorecard measures should be based on your customers' definition of quality. Figure 8-2 is a snapshot of the pdchange scorecard, and it demonstrates the cascading logic of quality measures, supporting performance indicators and proficiency levels.

Figure 8–2   pdchange Scorecard

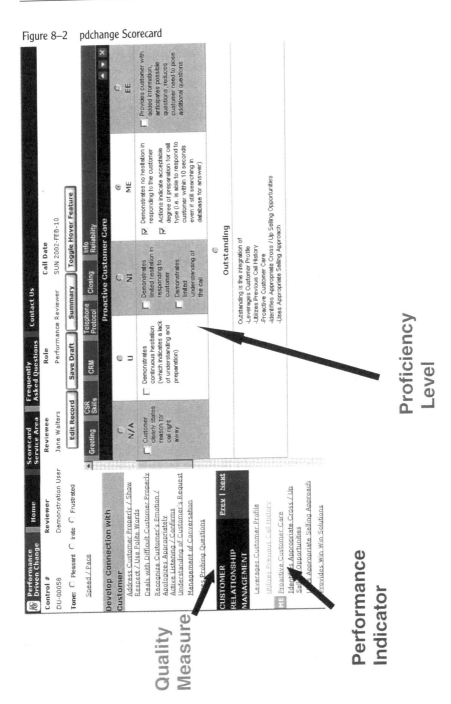

The pdchange scorecard is divided into six quality measures:
1. Greeting
2. CSR Communication Skills
3. Customer Relationship Management
4. Telephone Protocol
5. Closing
6. Information Reliability

Greetings

Greeting measures the first interaction between customers and customer service representatives (CSRs). The first impression created by employees is critical in setting the tone and expectation of quality for the entire interaction. When measuring standard greetings, look for whether the CSRs identify who the customer is, if they offer the customer assistance and what kind of tone is used.

CSR Communication Skills

CSR communication skills measures how CSRs manage calls, assess and manage the customers' needs, address the customers and deliver the information. This quality measure assesses skills and behaviors, which help cultivate a positive and trustworthy customer relationship.

Customer Relationship Management

Customer relationship management measures CSRs' ability to effectively use existing CRM tools (desktop application with customer profile and contact history), proactively identify customers' needs and deliver appropriate actions while providing appropriate solutions. This area also measures the effective use of customer information and contact history to limit the number of times customers have to repeat information from call to call (e.g., preferences, product holdings etc.) and to leverage existing customer information to increase customer loyalty and value by providing personalized service (right product/service, right time, right price).

Telephone Protocol

Telephone protocol measures CSRs' ability to manage the flow of conversations including holds and transfers. This section is designed to clarify expectations regarding the conversations and to avoid unpleasant disruptions. If calls are managed effectively, customers will be satisfied with the results, and costs savings, as a result of shorter talk times can be realized.

Closing

The closing measures the last phase of the interaction between the organization and its customers. This gives CSRs the chance to summarize and confirm a full understanding of the proposed solution, mutual expectations and next steps. It is also an opportunity to ensure that all of the customers' needs have been identified and satisfied. If managed appropriately, the closing should increase customer satisfaction and decrease the likelihood of callbacks.

Information Reliability

Information reliability measures the accuracy and completeness of the information provided to customers. If incorrect information is provided, the best that could happen is that customers call back to get clarification. However, more often than not, customers will not call back but will abandon the service.

COACHING AND EMPLOYEE PERFORMANCE AGREEMENTS

Since your employees are one of the most powerful ways of achieving quality service and your CRM vision, let's focus on them and determine how a Quality Service Performance Program can ensure they are mobilized and accountable. Aligning people and measuring and managing their performance are the key to achieving quality outcomes and, in turn, reaching and sustaining your client relationship management vision.

Many organizations have attempted to implement a comprehensive performance management program that incorporates a coaching program and employee performance agreements but with little success. This often fails due to lack of commitment and perseverance. Before you implement coaching and employee performance agreements, keep in mind that a successful implementation requires three factors:

1. A high level of management commitment to follow the program strictly and continue to ensure it is positive in nature. All too often, management is enthusiastic at the start but quickly moves the program to the bottom of the priority list as other "more important" issues come up. These managers fail to realize that employee performance is directly related to organizational performance, and nothing is more important than that.

2. A commitment by the organization to ensure the program is a positive and progressive one and not one that is negative in nature (either intentionally or not). This requires managers to be trained on how to coach, encourage performance improvement and reward staff properly. It also requires the organization to deal with nonperformers quickly and efficiently. Nothing discourages a high performer more quickly than no action being taken with intentional low performers.

3. A commitment to longevity. Improvements in performance take time. Some can be achieved quickly, but long-term, substantial improvements require time. Nothing is more demoralizing to employees than to launch a performance improvement program and then not to follow through until improvements can be realized (for example, employees are spoken to about their performance and are provided their scores, but the program is abandoned and employees never get a chance to demonstrate that they have improved.

What are some of the leading practices that a coaching and employee performance agreement program focused on quality service and continuous improvement should incorporate? Leading organizations ensure their coaching and employee performance agreement programs contain the following:

- a process of aligning individual performance goals with those of the organization

- a comprehensive and continuous approach for improving performance towards customers
- a set of practices and tools through which coaching is provided to employees, such as employee performance agreements (EPAs) and rewards and recognition
- a positive, not punitive focus—not a "gotcha" system, but a supportive learning development system
- helpful performance data (for both the organization and employees) that identify what works in various aspects of the program and what does not
- enabling mechanisms by defining, in detail, what is required for employees to do well
- a process for motivating and encouraging employees toward desired behaviors
- clear and unambiguous messages as to what is important to the organization and customers—a focus on addressing underlying issues not just symptoms

Coaching to Excellence is a route map that PwC Consulting has developed, incorporating leading coaching practices from various organizations. Our program is used to improve and optimize employee performance. It can be defined as the ongoing exchange of performance data results between employees and management. It is intended to sustain and improve employee performance and allow effective feedback and coaching, with a view to helping employees excel in their performance and encourages them to work toward the organization's CRM vision. It has two main components: coaching and the employee performance agreements (EPA). One of the tools used in this program to collect, measure and coach is the pdchange scorecard.

Coaching

The purpose of providing regular coaching to employees is to ensure that they are receiving focused direction on how to improve their performance and to provide positive reinforcement. The following pages provide you with the necessary criteria in building your own Coaching to Excellence program.

Constructive coaching must be given in such a way that it:

- reinforces correct behavior
- reinforces employee strengths
- corrects a problem by offering a constructive resolution
- develops skills required for the future
- offers specific suggestions for improvement
- solicits employee feedback
- considers individual staff needs and sense of self-worth
- provides positive and instructive support

Coaching sessions are very personal to employees. The sessions provide the opportunity to boost your employees' morale and to influence the best performance for the future. If done correctly, the sessions can have an immediate impact. If done incorrectly, the negative impact may never go away. When conducting coaching sessions, ensure that you do the following:

- Determine the purpose for the session prior to meeting with employees. Feedback can be provided for several reasons: praise, training, instructing, correcting.

- Have performance data available for discussion and ensure you have reviewed this information.

- Begin by communicating to employees that these sessions are intended to help them to improve.

- Listen to your employees and ask them to provide self-assessments. Then, provide your own assessment by beginning with a positive comment.

- Do not allow personal biases to play a part. Employees will notice and focus in on this.

- Do not allow past performance to influence the present. Focus on the future, and use past information only as a baseline against which to gauge improvement.

- Reward all efforts. Rewards should be consistent, known, frequent, meaningful and earned.

- Be regular and prompt in conducting formal/informal coaching sessions.

- Maintain confidentiality.

- Stick to the facts when discussing poor performance.

- Focus first on areas in which employees are performing well. Then, turn your attention to areas that require improvement. This reinforces positive behavior.
- Point out a customer's reaction to a performance.
- Determine the specific required actions together.

Coaching should be the process by which the organization makes each employee count as an individual participant and contributor. To do this, individual employee goals should be related to the performance driven CRM vision, and meaningful direction on how to achieve these must be provided. In the absence of meaningful direction (letting people know where they need to improve and how), employees will revert to traditional working habits, patterns and outdated customer management techniques.

When coaching, remember, each person is unique. Not all people are equal, but if you understand what motivates and drives your employees and how they approach their work and day-to-day life on an individual basis, then you will also be in a position to coach and direct them appropriately. The best way to get this information is to spend time with you staff members, get to know them and ask them these questions. Some employees may be dynamic and energetic but not focused, while others will be directional and focused but are not dynamic and high in energy. Still others will lack both energy and direction. The optimal combination for success a balance of high energy (scoring 8–10 points) and focus. These employees will be focused in direction and dynamic in their work. This analysis is illustrated in Figure 8-3.

Figure 8–3   Performance Analysis

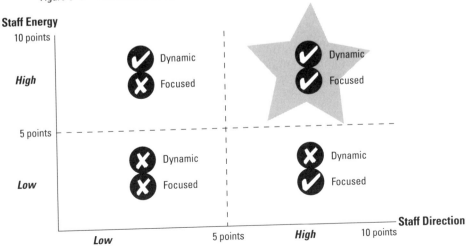

Employee Performance Agreements

Once employees have been aligned against the CRM vision, they understand their contribution and can visualize the endstate, employee performance agreements (EPAs) should be developed to ensure that employees continue on the right track, improve and reach their performance potential.

The purpose of an EPA is to promote a consistent method of enhancing the quality of work and maximizing an employee's potential in the organization. The EPA must be considered a mutual benefit for the employee and the organization to make it effective. The investments made in an employee should see a return in increased productivity, quality and overall commitment to the CRM vision.

The EPA is a living and continuously evolving document. The current EPA should build on the past ones, celebrating successes and identifying new strategies and opportunities. To be successful, performance should be measured throughout the year. EPAs cannot be a one-time event. To be meaningful and continuously improve, the employee must be empowered to manage his or her own performance within the boundaries set out and agreed to within the EPA throughout the year.

It is important that the EPA acts as an enabling tool, which introduces a structured and consistent process to having an open, honest, supportive and meaningful discussion about an employee's performance. The purpose of an EPA is to promote a consistent method of enhancing the quality of work and maximizing the employee's potential in the organization.

Employees should take the lead and primary responsibility to drive the EPA process. This is their agreement with the organization. They should view the EPA as a means to document, receive and obtain what is required to become and/or maintain being highly productive and valuable. The benefits to employees are increased job satisfaction, feelings of self-worth, being in control and receiving support from the organization.

But why does the EPA often fail? EPAs must be introduced into the organization slowly and with considerable support from management. The process requires a commitment of leadership and time. Most organizations that fail at introducing and maintaining EPAs fail because of the lack of required commitment in time and resources. The second most common reason organizations fail with their employee performance agreement attempts is that they are not really committed to using the process. This lack of commitment is demonstrated by the fact that the agreement becomes just another piece of paper that has to be completed once a year. Little time is spent on training staff on the EPA, and management does not communicate it as a priority. Your Organizational Performance Program should measure the commitment level to EPAs.

It is essential that an EPA be viewed as a proactive self-management tool, not as a management "stick." The organization must ensure a safe and professional environment for the first year that the EPA is introduced (e.g., do not tie compensation to the EPA for the first year). Key messages communicating that this is a proactive management tool aimed at empowering, actualizing and improving employees must be sent loudly and clearly (for example, through employee of the month awards). The EPA focuses employees on key value-added activities that are aligned with the CRM vision. Employees can see how they fit in and make a difference.

The first EPA is the most difficult to complete. The employee should have a sample completed EPA to help them complete theirs. The employee should be provided with the time and required support to review and understand the EPA, and a mutually agreed-to time and location should be set to complete their EPA. Employees should be provided with focused time to first complete their EPAs on their own, before they meet with the agreement holder. The time to complete the first EPA by the employee should take about half a day.

When implementing the EPAs, remember the following:

- The EPA process improves with experience, and a learning and implementation curve should be allowed for. Usually it takes one to two cycles to work very well.

- An EPA must be reviewed after six months by the employee and supervisor, and more frequently if possible. Employees should refer to their EPAs often to help keep them focused about their priorities and keep track of commitments made in their EPAs. Perhaps most importantly, employees should remember to note their performance and achievements continuously in order to celebrate their successes.

There are a number of critical success factors for building and implementing a highly useful EPA:

• The EPA should be viewed and supported as a proactive management tool by both employees and organization.

• A common understanding of the EPA purpose, language and definitions should be achieved.

• Performance expectations, accountabilities, responsibilities and commitments for both employees and the organization should be commonly understood.

• Sufficient time should be allowed to learn and effectively implement the EPA process.

• The EPA should be completed in a mutually agreed-to private time and location.

• The contents of the EPA should be mutually agreed to by employees and the organization.

• Employees must be responsible for their day-to-day ongoing self-assessment and performance evaluation.

• The EPA should be completed fully every 12 months. A formal review should occur, at a minimum, every six months. More frequent reviews are encouraged. If there is a significant change in responsibilities or the EPA in general, a new EPA should be completed, still building on the existing one whenever possible.

• Key commitments should be specific and appropriate to the position, level, and role in the organization. Opportunities can reflect employees' desire to move outside of their normal position, level and role.

• Performance measures should be within the performer's control. They should be specific, meaningful, realistic, timely, valid, clear and measurable.

• All employees must believe that they are being treated equitably.

• The formal system does not replace the day-to-day supervisory responsibilities of providing ongoing feedback to employees.

• There should be no surprises for employees at the formal review periods. The formal review should be a confirmation of what is already known.

Below is a sample EPA from our Coaching to Excellence program.

EMPLOYEE PERFORMANCE AGREEMENT TEMPLATE

Employee Performance Agreement Statement

This section states in a clear and succinct manner the overall focus and intent of employees over the next year. Employees should include an overall statement of achievement: what they want to work toward, their objectives and their personal commitments.

Achievement Statement

A specific statement of what will be achieved should be included in this section. The statement should read as an employee "CRM vision." For example, the achievement statement may be: "Over the next year, I will ensure that my responsibilities are performed in an effective, efficient and quality manner. My focus will be on improving my CRM skills. I want to ensure a high-level of quality and commitment to my customers. I will explore new opportunities in order to expand my current customer service skill set. In order to do this, I will participate proactively in corporate priorities and seek out new opportunities. This commitment is represented in my learning plan."

Objectives

Overall employee objectives should be included in this section. The objectives should be general in nature covering the broad range of functions and responsibilities the employee may have. Example objectives are:

- To enhance my performance continually in the areas of quality call service.
- To be recognized as a valuable and contributing employee in achieving our CRM vision.
- To provide professional, quality, timely and valued services internally and externally.

Personal Commitments

This section includes the personal attributes and contributions the employee intends to demonstrate and achieve. Examples of personal commitments are as follows:

- To demonstrate personal commitment and professionalism in all interactions with my customers.

- To cultivate positive internal/external relationships.

- To obtain/incorporate required training into day-to-day work for the purpose of enhancing performance.

- To be committed to being a team player.

Details of Employee Core CRM Activities

This section describes in detail what the employee will be responsible for. A description of how this responsibility aligns itself with the employee's overall CRM vision should be included. Key customer segments, outcomes and performance measures should also be detailed in this section for each area of responsibility.

Enough information should be contained so that if an "outsider" was to read this section, he or she would understand *what* the employee does and *how it aligns* with the overall CRM vision.

Strategies for Achievement

Strategies describe how employees intend to achieve what they have committed to over the period covered by the employee performance agreement. This description includes the level and details of the support/commitments required by employees of the organization (e.g., upraded technology, quality service training).

Performance Outcomes and Measures

This details how employees and the organization will know if the employees were successful. How will "success" be defined? What do employees need to keep track of to demonstrate their success? The performance outcomes and measures should be defined as a combination of "inputs," "outputs" and "outcomes." Expected standards, outcomes and time lines should be documented and agreed to. In order to ensure continuous improvement, this section should include a review of the previous year's standards and targets. Each year, this area should build onto the previous year. Performance outcomes and measures should be specific, meaningful, realistic, clear and valid.

Key Customers

Key Customers to be serviced should be included in this section. This enables employees to keep their "customer service" focus clear and up front. This also helps to identify priorities for the employees.

Employee Learning Plan

This section should include employees' learning objectives over the next year. Strategies, commitments and required supports/enablers should be listed. It is important for the organization to commit the required supports, which in turn will enable employees to achieve success. Completing this section ensures that employees are able to access the required learning to meet their overall and detailed objectives, strategies and commitments. Included should be all the "mandatory" required training resulting from new policies, programs or technology improvements.

Learning Objectives and Strategies

Employees' learning objectives should be detailed in this section. All forms of training should be explored (e.g., workshops, tutorials, multimedia). Personal/professional capacity enhancements should also be included, and a description of how this will benefit the overall organization should be detailed. Possible transferring of knowledge learned should be explored. For example, once employees are trained they agree to act as trainers for other employees.

Learning Measures

Expected learning outcomes and measures should be detailed in this section. How will employees and the agreement holders know if the employees are successful? How will "success" be defined? What do employees need to keep track of to demonstrate their success? The learning measures should be defined as a combination of "inputs," "outputs" and "outcomes." Expected standards, outcomes and time lines should be documented and agreed to.

Performance Summary

KEY COMMITMENTS	KEY PERFORMANCE MEASURE	KEY RESULTS ACHIEVED

GENERAL AREA OF MEASUREMENT	SPECIFIC COMMENTS
Overall quality of work	
Productivity	
Meeting deadlines	
Adherence to policies and procedures	
Communication skills— verbal and written	
Initiative/motivation	
Taking personal responsibility	
Planning/organizing capability	
Interpersonal relations	
Team player	
Adaptability	

GENERAL AREA OF MEASUREMENT	SPECIFIC COMMENTS
Reliability—attendance and punctuality	
Judgment	
Leadership qualities	
Decision-making ability	
Management/supervisory skills (if applicable)	

Achievements

Celebrate Success! Additional staff achievements should be described and highlighted in this section. They should reference the meeting or exceeding of commitments. Any additional responsibilities—including projects, assisting other staff, special assignments etc.—should be profiled.

Rewards and Recognitions

Rewards and recognitions should be listed in this section. Rewards may include salary increases, agreement to participate in a limited training and/or conference opportunity. Recognitions may include lunch with the CAO, profile in the staff newsletter, recommendation for promotion etc.

The EPA should serve as a proactive quality and capacity building tool—a tool that ensures effective communication between employees and the organization. Completing an EPAP should result in several benefits, as outlined in Table 8-1 below:

Benefits for the Employee	Benefits for the Organization
– improved accountability	– improved accountability
– clear expectations and responsibilities	– clear expectations and responsibilities
– an understanding of how they "fit in"	– an understanding of how they "fit in"
– a proactive means to improvement	– improved quality of work
– a honest discussion around performance	– a fair and open performance process
– rewards and recognition	– satisfied employees
– opportunties in interest areas	– empowered employees
– sense of purpose	– enhanced ability to achieve objectives
– increased productivity	– sense of control
– sense of self-worth	– enhanced organizational credibility

Table 8-1

Creating a Positive Experience

A positive experience will go a long way in trying to improve your staff's performance. Management may not be able to control everything in a coaching session, but if the following suggestions are followed, it will improve the coaching program. There are a number of things you can do to create a positive Coaching to Excellence experience. Try some of these:

- Celebrate successes early in the process.
- Find opportunities to generate some immediate successes or positive feedback.
- Encourage staff members to use improvement tools provided by the organization in their everyday actions.

- Fully support the implementation of a program such as this one whatever that program is in your organization.

- Offer praise to those who have successfully embraced performance improvement.

- Communicate positively and honestly with staff.

- Meet with all staff on a regular basis.

- Develop several communications and feedback strategies (e.g., staff meetings, rumor box, bulletin boards etc.) to encourage staff input.

SELF-ASSESSMENT TOOL

As many organizations begin to develop and implement a Quality Service Performance Program, they find that they cannot take full advantage of the potential benefits of such a program. There are a number of road blocks the OPP must be maneuvered it's way around. These road blocks can also be referred to as platforms organizations reach, and often remain in, when implementing a Quality Service Performance Program. To be successful, you must move from platform to platform. There are three platforms an organization can plateau on:

- Framework Platform—A framework is developed and not implemented.

- Measurement Platform—The framework is implemented, and measures are developed. Performance data is being collected, but it is not used to manage and change.

- Management Platform—Performance data is being collected, and has started to be used, but continuous improvement is not being practiced.

A self-assessment tool can capture how well your QSPP is doing and whether you are maximizing the benefits of your program. Complete the self-assessment on the next page to determine which platform you have reached.

Do You Have the Following?	Yes	Platform Reached
A well-defined description of the principles, process and criteria for the Quality Service Performance Program.		Framework platform
Defined continuous improvement process.		
Strong organizational leadership and commitment to measuring performance.		
Defined quality measures with supporting performance indicators and proficiency ratings.		Measurement platform
Quality service measures that have been aligned with the CRM vision.		
A measurement process for collecting performance data (e.g., a scorecard).		
A combination of various monitoring activities that have been implemented.		
A calibration process, sample plan and designed management information reports.		
A third-party validation process.		
A culture of using performance information to manage the organization—a clear picture of performance is being painted, and there is a commitment to, and excitement around, the performance program.		Management platform
Measures that are focused on CRM outcomes not inputs/outputs.		

Once you have determined which platform you have reached, take one of the self-assessment quizzes below to determine what risks you face.

Your Framework Is	Yes	No	What Is Your Risk?
Easily understood.			If no, you may be at risk
Easy to operate in.			of plateauing on the frame-
An excellent communication tool.			work platform.
Translated into actions.			If no, then you may be
Implementable and realistic.			at risk of plateauing on the measurement platform.
Intimidating or nonthreatening to individuals.			
Directly linked to individual performance.			
Clear on who the measurement owners are.			

Your Measurements Are	Yes	No	What Is Your Risk?
Visible in their benefits to the organization.			If no, you may be at risk of plateauing on the manage-
User friendly.			ment platform.
Consistently defined and understood.			
Resulting in the right performance data.			
Relying on various data collection and reporting tools.			
Demonstrating that the effort to collect the data is valuable and effective.			

How Can You Move Forward?

What can you do about moving forward? To move from the framework platform to the measurement platform, you must first communicate effectively the measures to all employees and demonstrate how the framework will be translated into performance measures. Further, you must demonstrate how each measure will align with each critical component of your CRM vision. The value of the Quality Service Performance Program must also be demonstrated. Answer your staff: How will implementing the framework add to CRM improvement?

Secondly, you must reestablish and demonstrate through specific activity the continued commitment to measuring quality service. One of the most influential actions is to dedicate resources to translating the framework into reality.

To move from the measurement platform, your audience must now be secured. This can be accomplished by positioning the Quality Service Performance Program as a positive and proactive tool. This is not as easily done as said. There is a long history of viewing performance measurement as a punitive, reactive means of weeding out the good from the bad. To move from this negative to the positive, which is absolutely required to make any gains in your CRM vision, start small and identify early QSSP wins. This will assist with gaining enthusiasm and cooperation. In addition, develop a solid, realistic but challenging, phased-in implementation plan that is supported by practical and useful enabling supports.

If you are measuring, you already have performance information and data. The challenge is to ensure that you have the right data and that the value of using this data is understood. The organization should not begin to use performance data until there is assurance that the data is valid, useful and accurate. Validation must be obtained to ensure that the right information is being collected. You can also assist in moving from the measurement platform to the management platform by doing the following:

- Ensure that consistent terminology is being used.
- Collect only the information that you need to paint a picture of quality service.
- Do not collect unnecessary information.
- Develop a regular reporting process that enhances accountability.

- Communicate success, and demonstrate how performance information is being used.

When you reach the management platform, reward yourself. Although the concept of managing with performance data is not new, many organizations have not yet achieved this platform. Answer the following questions to see if you are on this platform:

- Have you implemented your Quality Service Performance Program framework?

- Are you employing performance measurement techniques?

- Is performance data being collected and reported, and are you using this data to drive future change and requirements?

If you are able to answer yes to the above three questions, you may be wondering what the next step is. An organization must move beyond the management platform because remaining there does not allow for a commitment to continuous improvement. Continuous improvement occurs when the performance data is used to cycle back to the original CRM vision to ensure that all the components related to providing quality service are being met and are still relevant. When this happens you are practising performance driven CRM.

SUMMARY

As in the other performance programs, information is critical. For an organization to fully implement a Quality Service Performance Program, which is committed to continuous improvement, care and attention must be given to the following three areas:

1. Continuous Improvement Framework and Quality Scorecard—The framework, which is built around the scorecard, sets expectations and measures and provides the basis for coaching and training.

2. Coaching and Employee Performance Agreements—The coaching program encourages staff performance improvement and aligns staff behaviors and responsibilities with your CRM vision. It must be a positive and proactive method for providing employee feedback on performance. An employee performance agreement process/template supports effective communication of accountabilities, requirements and achievement between the employee and organization.

3. Self-Assessment Tool—This tool captures how well your QSPP is doing and whether you are maximizing the benefits of your program.

All of these collectively contribute to the totality of the Quality Service Performance Program (QSPP). But remember, that while there are a number of tools and technologies to support an Organizational Performance Program and to help manage workload, scheduling and training, that there are very few that will fully assist with the QSPP. The primary method for achieving and continuously improving quality service must be through a well-developed and comprehensive quality-monitoring program. Technologies exist to support or enable quality monitoring and improvement (for example, call taping equipment to monitor calls), but few technology enablers exist to actually complete the quality monitoring.

Part Four

Leading Practices in Creating Performance Driven CRM

O V E R V I E W

Companies across the globe face the same challenge: competition is more aggressive, and differentiation is more difficult to achieve. Firms that were once concerned only with national competition face new market concerns that extend far beyond their country's borders. Competition has reached global proportions, and businesses are realizing that winning strategies depend on more than lowering prices. As markets become increasingly commodity-based, succeeding in the global game requires a strategy that will set companies apart from their competition.

Through our work with various organizations, we have recognized that some companies were having tremendous success in improving customer satisfaction, while others seemed to be losing market share by neglecting the Customer Relationship Management (CRM) edge. Over the years, we have noticed a number of changes and shifts. In reality, there are some fundamental differences between companies that have achieved improved performance, customer loyalty and retention and those that have been less than successful in satisfying their customers. Many of these have been described in various chapters throughout this book, and we will point you back to these on occasion.

But there is more. Our research suggests a number of key practices followed by companies that have been successful. These practices are fundamentally described in Part Two of this book and center around fully functional programs such as the following:

- Customer Performance Program (CPP), which ensures that an ongoing understanding of the customer is achieved

- Organizational Performance Program (OPP), which ensures an ongoing understanding of its own organization

- Quality Service Performance Program (QSPP), which ensures an ongoing commitment to continuous improvement in quality service

These practices are not novel. It's the manner in which they are implemented that is critical, and thus, this is the purpose of the tools and techniques described in the chapters in Part Three.

Now it is time to start on your journey to create performance driven CRM. Consider the following:

- What are your core competencies?
- Have you laid the foundation for the requisite performance programs?
- Do you understand which tools and technology are required to enable the CPP, OPP and QSPP?
- Are you committed to performance driven CRM and the measurement prerequisites?

Before you proceed, consider the impact of the Internet and customer contact center on your business environment and the critical synergy that must be created between the Customer Performance Program (CPP) and the Quality Service Performance Program (QSPP). The nature of business is changing rapidly. The use of the Internet and of Internet-based technologies is shaping how business is conducted around the world. The new business environment requires organizations to rethink their approach to dealing with their customers.

The integration of the customer contact center and the Internet into day-to-day organizational operations represents one of the key emerging trends in the twenty-first century economy. The impact is such that contact centers are expected to affect almost all aspects of society—from the private sector to public sector—in all parts the world. To do this, they must first develop a deeper understanding of all points of interaction with the customer (the CPP), whether the contact is inbound from the customer, outbound from the organization or via the telephone, mail, web, e-mail, a set-top box or a combination of these.

Multimedia, multichannel customer contact centers are at the heart of this changing relationship and are key enablers for companies looking to meet this new challenge. Customers want to contact companies at their (the customers) convenience, using the most convenient means. Good service (through the QSPP) is now a survival issue, and the battle is being fought over the perceived value that customers receive from their relationship with their suppliers.

Chapter 9 will provide you with a framework for considering performance driven CRM in a multichannel environment and synergistically linking the CPP and QSPP. To be competitive in today's dynamic global marketplace, organizations need to adopt a multichannel approach toward Customer Relationship Management (CRM) and incorporate it completely into their business. That brings new pressures on the critical performance programs (Part Two) and the tools and technology (Part Three) required to propel performance driven CRM.

CRM is about customer knowledge—collecting, accessing, analyzing and acting on knowledge of the customer to give more personal and professional service. It is about better managing the enterprise around customer interactions and maximizing the lifetime value of customer relationships. It is about using the company's knowledge of its customers in a consistent and uniform way across all departments and functions. And with it, comes the need for new competencies and enabling technology.

But all your efforts will be suboptimal unless you understand and embrace that in order to be successful, performance driven CRM must involve your staff. This involvement means the following:

- Give your staff CRM vision direction that they can all see and understand. Make it real for them through clearly articulated expectations and targets that are part of the CRM vision.
- Build on the QSPP, and demonstrate to staff through performance coaching and reward programs what each individual does that contributes to success.

By bringing staff to their full potential, the organization is brought to its full potential, which, in turn, means being in a position to realize your CRM vision. Thus the purpose of Chapter 10. This chapter will provide you with that extra guidance and a workbook to map your personal plan. Focusing on the employee and employee satisfaction and growth is the key to success. But it must be recognized that success can be derived only from a combination of attitude, performance and behavior. If an organization can motivate staff to have the right attitude, the right performance and the right behavior, it will be successful at achieving its CRM vision. To accomplish this, the organization (meaning all people, processes, policies and operations) has to also have the right attitude, performance and behavior.

Chapter 10 provides some key guideposts that are built on four main components.

1. The first component is beginning the performance improvement journey. Here employees must understand what motivates them

to improve. Is it for the right reasons? Are they committed to improving?

2. The second component, planning the route, is the one in which staff members plan their destination. They set the route to improve.

3. The third component is staying the course by making the investment in self and starting to take action.

4. The final component is to ensure success by staying focused, adopting a concept of managing upward and practicing continuous self-improvement.

If followed correctly, this should alter your staff's attitudes and your company's ability to achieve performance driven CRM.

If you have accomplished this, and before you set out on your journey, you should consider our concluding chapter. In Chapter 11, we provide you with some lessons learned from those who failed and a reference back to previous chapters of the book to offer up solutions. Whether your organization is about to embark on a new initiative to deliver performance driven CRM or it requires a bit of fine-tuning, we think that you will find these examples an effective guide. The chapter provides some tips to ensure that your performance driven CRM initiative does not fail. The issues are not unique to any one industry or size of company but there is one common thread: to be successful a focus on standards, measurement and facts will drive success. And that is why performance driven CRM is absolutely critical.

And also remember, you'll face a number of obstacles as you embark toward performance driven CRM. With the route map found in the previous chapters, you will succeed, provided you meet the challenges ahead of you with resolve and commitment.

The performance driven CRM model might seem to you as if it were just common sense. Perhaps. But as Voltaire said, "If common sense were very common, more people would have more of it."

Linking the Customer Performance Program and the Quality Service Performance Program

While all performance programs must be integrated in order to implement performance driven CRM, there is critical synergy that must be created between the Customer Performance Program (CPP) and the Quality Service Performance Program (QSPP). The CPP ensures an ongoing understanding of the customer, and the QSPP ensures an ongoing commitment to continuous improvement in quality service. Customer knowledge, by itself, is important, but it is only half the equation and incomplete unless the organization is also deeply committed to the delivery of quality service.

This new business environment requires organizations to rethink their approach to dealing with their customers. To do this, they must first develop a deeper understanding of all points of interaction with their customers, whether the contact is inbound from the customer, outbound from the organization or via the telephone, mail, the Web, e-mail, a set-top box or a combination of these. Whatever the nature or point of contact, customers want a seamless interaction throughout their experience with the company. And that puts extra pressure on the three performance programs. Customers expect companies to link all functions together into one integrated whole. Companies that succeed in doing this reap enormous benefits—as does everyone who conducts business with them. Customers receive a more personalized experience, while the company itself can now provide a consistent message across all customer interactions. This allows the company to turn proactively every interaction into an opportunity to build brand loyalty. This allows an organization to acquire, retain and grow customers and to build competitive advantage at a time of increased economic uncertainty, brought on by additional global pressures with the advent of e-business and the Internet.

ROLE OF THE INTERNET

The Internet has led to the creation of a customer base, which is more knowledgeable, demanding and less brand-loyal than ever before. Customers will not only browse and shop in an e-store, make online transactional decisions, request information and check order status online, but they will also demand to maintain traditional methods of interaction.

Analysis of leading companies has shown consistently that the top achievers of sustainable and profitable revenue growth have excelled in at least one of three key performance areas:

1. customer relationships

2. products and services

3. channels

The ultimate goal is to deliver the customer's preferred product through the most cost-effective channel—which is not only the preferred channel of the customer, but also the one that provides the best balance of cost efficiency and relationship building for the selling company. That's what Radio Shack Canada realized early on.

CASE STUDY
Radio Shack Canada

Radio Shack Canada, Canada's largest and most trusted consumer electronics retailer, recognized that in order to achieve performance driven CRM, it was critical to be in a position to balance its CPP with its QSPP through a multimedia contact center environment. It firmly believed that beyond sales and support, customer service and satisfaction were paramount goals that could not be ignored in today's business world.

In-store and catalog sales have been the mainstay of Radio Shack Canada's business since 1970. But with the proliferation of the Internet in all aspects of daily life, the company realized that it could improve its reach, offerings and service by adding and integrating a new channel—the Internet—to interact with customers 24 hours a day, seven days a week. With an online presence, it could improve its CPP and deliver an enhanced QSPP, and thus establish performance driven CRM.

Here's how. On the CPP front, customer-centric companies such as Radio Shack Canada are always searching for ways to achieve higher customer satisfaction and retention, higher revenues per customer and lower costs for acquiring and servicing customers. Radio Shack Canada's goal was to get to know its customers better, wherever they should happen to be located—at home or at a Radio Shack Canada store—and it was able to do that by integrating the customer knowledge obtained through the online store with that available from its traditional channels. This new database stored product and customer information, interacting quickly, efficiently and securely with Radio Shack Canada's wired customers and existing business applications. Once launched, the site offered visitors access to thousands of products, most major brands and a huge selection of electronic equipment and accessories.

To complement its Web strategy, Radio Shack Canada also chose to offer an additional variation on this channel: Internet-enabled, in-store kiosks in all if its corporate locations. This strategy weds the online and offline marketplaces by giving consumers the choice to shop from home and have their products shipped directly to them or visit and buy from their local Radio Shack Canada stores, allowing the company to build better relationships—a key performance measure within its QSPP. These relationships with its customers were enhanced not just by responding to their needs, but also by anticipating them. The company can now answer its customers' questions 24/7, providing better customer service on a national scale.

As we stated earlier, to achieve performance driven CRM and true integration of the CPP and QSPP, an organization must excel in at least one of three key performance areas:

1.   customer relationships

2.   products and services

3.   channels

The ultimate goal is to deliver the customer's preferred product through the most cost-effective channel—which is not only the preferred channel of the customer, but also the one which provides the best balance of cost efficiency and relationship building for the selling company. Radio Shack Canada excelled in all three areas and is using this newfound customer information to create improved quality service delivery, continuous improvement and lasting performance driven CRM .

On a different twist on the same theme, the example that follows shows how knowing your customers, and what is important to them (the CPP), using channel technology (again the Internet) and being prepared to be monitored and managed by a strict QSPP can achieve customer loyalty and lasting CRM. As a backdrop, remember that creating lasting, performance driven customer relationships depends on building trust. Success will result in winning a larger share of the customer's lifetime value. The case that follows is not a business-to-business (b2b) example nor really a business-to-consumer (b2c) example: rather, it is a good example on how an organization can achieve trust. It's a demonstration on how an organization can use multiple channels (face-to-face and the Internet) to provide its customers with assurance that it is looking after its most valuable assets. It shows that when a organization is prepared to be measured by its quality service performance standards (the QSPP), derived through an understanding of the customer (the CPP), true performance driven CRM will result.

CASE STUDY
Kids r Kids

Kids r Kids is a day-care center. When parents enroll their children in this facility, they are given a URL to access a particular Web site. The Web site is hosted by the organization, but what does it show? There are cameras throughout the facility, and when you log on to the Web site, you are given access to your children at play. You can observe how your assets are being cared for, and you can have access to this site any time of the working day. Log on for a few minutes and then log off, and go back to your own day-to-day activities.

Do you think that a level of trust has been established? Of course it has. The question for you is how do you embrace technology to allow your customers to have that same level of trust in you? How effective is your CPP? Do you know what it will take to achieve trust? How disciplined is your QSPP? Are you prepared to be measured on it by your customers?

ROLE OF THE MULTIMEDIA, MULTICHANNEL CONTACT CENTER

While the above has focused mainly on the Internet, it is only one of many channels that must be integrated to deliver performance driven CRM. Customers want to contact your company how they want, when they want and for what they want. And it is important that you measure your ability to deliver this in both your CPP and QSPP. Good service is the key differentiator—a survival issue—and the battle is being fought over the perceived value that customers receive from their relationship with their suppliers.

Companies must recognize the power of customers and their need for quality service and respond to it. Multimedia, multichannel customer contact centers are at the heart of this changing relationship and are a key for companies looking to meet this new challenge. So, let's step back for a minute and put traditional call centers and multichannel contact centers into perspective and then understand how and where this linkage of CPP and QSPP creates strategic advantage and lasting, performance driven CRM.

Here are the definitions provided by IDC, a reputed IT research group:

Traditional Call Centre

A call center is defined as a dedicated facility equipped with specialized communication equipment capable of handling large volumes of both inbound and outbound telephone calls. Call centers handle various types of customer interaction activities such as sales, financial transactions, order entry, billing enquiries, account maintenance, support service, dispatch, scheduling, general information, technical support etc. Some key technologies in call centers include private branch exchanges (PBXs), automated call distributors (ACDs), interactive voice response systems (IVRs), computer telephony integration software (CTI), call management software, customer interaction applications, voice recognition and natural language, knowledge bases etc.

MultiChannel Contact Centers

The traditional call center is currently evolving into what should more accurately be call the "customer contact center." Technological development (the Internet being a primary factor) and changing market needs are essentially transitioning call centers from a corporate operational cost center into a strategically significant business process. The focus is changing from handling customer calls to maximizing customer value through meaningful interaction. Furthermore, call centers are no longer just about calls. The growth of e-business has meant that an increasing number of call centers are equipping their facilities with technology capable of handling various modes of communication—such as fax, e-mail and Internet—in both live-agent and automated formats. These communication channels are often integrated with databases throughout the enterprise, which contain various types of customer information. Cost and efficiency considerations will drive the market further in the direction of adopting customer contact centers.

Multichannel customer contact is key to a CRM strategy focusing on the customer experience, across the entire customer lifecycle. But as highlighted in Part Three, new tools and methodologies are required to enable new processes that touch the customer. Consider the following stages in customer care—the stages that move us from customer acquisition to customer retention and the technologies and practices within the CPP that are critical:

- customer acquisition (and with it, the need for data warehousing, data mining, campaign management capabilities)
- developing business (through the use of telesales, remote sales, cross-selling, upselling)
- retention (and the need for loyalty schemes, personalization, win-back programs, problem resolution)

The multichannel customer contact center is fundamental to delivering on the QSPP in this two-way, valued and valuable customer relationship. As reported in a January 2001 PwC Consulting white paper entitled, *The Multimedia Customer Contact Center for Customer Relationship Management: The Changing Face of Customer Contact*, the nature of business is changing rapidly. The use of the Internet and of Internet-based technologies is shaping how business is conducted around the world as we move into the twenty-first century. To be competitive in today's dynamic global marketplace, organizations need to adopt a multichannel approach toward Customer Relationship Management (CRM) and incorporate it completely into their business. And that brings new pressures on the three performance programs (Part Two)—CPP, OPP and QSPP—and the tools to enable the performance programs (Part Three).

TECHNOLOGY—INCREASING CUSTOMER VALUE AND PROFITS

As highlighted in Part Three, as the scope of CRM increases through growth in the number and types of customer interactions, technology becomes a critical enabler. CRM package applications, described earlier in Chapter 6, provide functionality ranging from marketing and campaign management to remote sales and service to customer care and agent support within the customer contact center. These applications are themselves becoming increasingly Web-enabled, but they need to be integrated with a number of additional technologies and application functions in order to provide quality performance driven CRM. These include:

- personalization—the ability, based on and effective CPP, to personalize the Web site that the customer will access

- Web collaboration—the ability to chat online with the customer and provide assistance, when required, thereby enhancing the QSPP

- e-mail response management—the ability to respond to a customer's e-mail instantaneously, without human intervention

- integrated management of queues for voice, mail, fax/Web and e-mail—the ability to give high-value customers preferential treatment, regardless of which channel they use to communicate or interact with you

- voice-over IP—the ability to talk to the customer over the same Internet line

- voice recognition and processing—instead of pushing the telephone keypad to direct you to the right information or agent, the ability to speak directly into the telephone and have your words recognized

- Wireless Application Protocol (WAP) devices and servers—the ability to use your cellphone or palm-type device to communicate directly with the database within the supplier organization, to possibly place an order, obtain information or check order status

But it is not just technology—it is the right technology for the right customer. While some channels may be more cost efficient, they may not be more effective. Hence, the need exists for performance measurement and performance driven CRM.

CRM systems and suites can now seamlessly address both the traditional interaction channels (voice, face-to-face, mail) and also the e-sales, service and marketing aspects. Data warehousing and data mining tools (a key requirement for the CPP and an effective QSPP) enable comprehensive reporting on this 360-degree view of the customer as information is fed to and from the contact center. This data can be used to further the development of unique customer interactions through segmentation and customer profiling, which focuses and refines the customer interaction. Integration of this information provides full access to all customer information by all company divisions and enables the creation of personalized business development and retention programs. Web pages, automated voice service menus and product offerings are tailored to the profile of the individual customer and recent customer experiences, thereby enhancing the QSPP capabilities. Additional information regarding individual customer service interactions, a customer's preferences and individual customer behaviors (including behavior on the Web) can be captured at all customer touch points, analyzed and transformed into customer intelligence for use in the CPP. This can then be used for programs of one-to-one marketing, sales, service and care.

THE GLUE THAT ENABLES PERFORMANCE DRIVEN CRM

Computer telephony integration (CTI) is one technological tool for increasing customer satisfaction at a reduced cost. With CTI, customers are routed through the organization in a way that is based on a set of criteria appropriate to that organization's business (the CPP)—such as their market segment, the skill set of the customer contact agent, customer profile attributes and transactional need. Highly valued customers can be routed directly to an agent familiar with their needs. Less strategic or lower-valued customers who tend to have simpler, less complex requests can be routed to automated services and referred to the organization's Web site for self-service. This routing can be achieved for a number of different media types such as voice calls, Webcalls, e-mails and faxes.

Middleware solutions (termed such because they sit between the legacy systems and the front-end CRM applications) such as CTI can enhance customer interactions and agent productivity by enabling the integration of customer facing channels with legacy or back-office applications. As channels of customer contact multiply in response to the increasing e-business capabilities, the need for cross-channel integration becomes more urgent. Customers shop and place orders via the e-store, customer contact centers and sales force, but completion of sales transactions and inquiries is crucially dependent on interactions with key legacy applications: order fulfillment, inventory and logistics. Middleware provides the mechanism for ensuring that up-to-the-minute customer activity information is made available to all channels, ensuring a successful and consistent customer experience, as you will see in the examples that follow.

Remember, the CPP is about customer knowledge: collecting, accessing, analyzing and acting on knowledge of the customer to give more personal and professional service (the QSPP). It is about better managing the enterprise around customer interactions and maximizing the lifetime value of customer relationships. It is about using the company's knowledge of its customers in a consistent and uniform way across all departments and functions. Customer analytic tools such as data warehousing and decision support solutions (as referenced in the description of data mining models in Chapter 6) are quickly becoming the backbone for effectively managing and analyzing the tremendous amounts of customer profiles and transactional data being captured through the interaction channels. More organizations are feeling the heat to better integrate and leverage customer information and service across channels. This is due primarily to the visible success of some business enterprises along these lines, ever-expanding technical possibilities and growing speed-to-market pressure to develop products and services and to improve customer service. Customer analytic tools allow companies to leverage inference-based data with data gathered in realtime to further customize offers to customers while providing consistent messages to customers across all channels.

THE CASE FOR INTEGRATED CPP AND QSPP

We have assisted many organizations in the enterprise-wide design and integration of customer contact centers that maximizes customer satisfaction and retention and is aligned with the company's targeted business strategy and CRM vision. Not surprisingly, the design is based on an ability to derive and monitor on the basis of the CPP and QSPP and to use that for continuous improvement and as input to the Organizational Performance Program (OPP). This design of the target CRM environment must therefore incorporate strategic, organization and process change and should be underpinned by integrated customer contact center technologies, which enable multimedia customer contact.

Below, we provide three scenarios taken from this work. Each one highlights certain capabilities, performance driven CRM-required competencies, potential benefits and enabling technology. Read the examples and then, at the end of each case, review the summary provided.

CASE STUDY 1

How Important Are You?
Customer Value Routing and Cross-Sell
on Voice Service Call

It has been reported that a customer is five times more likely to respond favorably to a cross-sell or upsell solicitation, after his or her service request has been satisfied, than to an outbound telemarketing request. Think about it, are you not more likely to be favorably disposed to organizations or individuals after they have provided you with some level of assistance? Consider this scenario.

A customer that has just purchased a new home computer places a call to the customer contact center with a service problem—one of the software applications is not working. The customer places a call to the customer service department, responds to an interactive voice response (IVR) prompt for the type of inquiry and enters the appropriate selection for "service" on the phone. The customer is also prompted for and provides his customer ID number on the phone. (The customer has already pre-registered his computer, the peripheral equipment that was purchased and the total configuration of his business office. Based on this, the organization has qualified him as a high-value customer and assigned him a special ID number.)

Because of his high value to the organization, the customer is routed to a designated specialist that is most knowledgeable in this computer configuration. When the service specialist accepts the call, she receives through the computer telephony intergration (CTI) application, a screen pop-up containing contact history information and all previous service requests logged for the customer in a customized service view. All customer enquiries must be logged in the CRM customer management application to ensure that a proper history of the customer is kept. The service specialist opens a new service request, again through the CRM application, in order to log the problem. The service specialist then searches the solutions database for the most appropriate solution to resolve the problem. Once the appropriate solution has been given to the customer, the specialist can save this solution within the customer's service request.

Assuming that this does provide the appropriate fix, the service specialist can now close the service request. During the wrap-up for this call, the service specialist offers the customer a campaign that has been targeted for him by the marketing department (in this case, a special Internet service at a substantially reduced introductory price). The customer requests product information before responding to the campaign. The customer service representative (CSR) uses the detailed product information pages on the customer relationship portal to fulfill the customer's inquiry on product features and price. The customer requests the service, the fulfillment request is forwarded to the marketing department and the call is ended.

But that is not all. A random selection of the calls received by this CSR are monitored for quality, accuracy and completeness of call. Once a week, the supervisor and agent review the QSPP standards and the CSR's delivery against these standards. Where appropriate, customized coaching and training are scheduled.

This scenario shows us the following:

- the importance of the CPP, and why segmentation and customer information profiling can be used to personalize the customer experience

- critical tools to enable the CPP—IVR, CTI, data warehousing and data mining

- the need for a QSPP to ensure that quality service is provided to the customer

CASE STUDY 2

Picking the Right Channel to Meet Customer Needs—e-Store Channel Integration

Some customers do not want to travel to order the products and services they require. The Internet, of course, provides that alternative but has also created a more knowledgeable, discerning and price-conscious consumer—one who requires customer-friendly interaction and quality service delivery. And as far as that customer service delivery goes, even though the customer is conducting business over the Web, the contact center will still play a critical role. Here's how.

A customer browses a computer Web site in order to research the various products offered in the e-store. She decides that she is interested in purchasing one of the computer models offered there. She creates a shopping basket for the desired products and enters the appropriate quantities for each product model, resulting in a quote for the package of goods requested. After selecting all desired products for the quote, she saves the quote with a unique name, let's say "My Computer," so that she can find it again easily. The customer browses a number of other Web sites and finds that this first company provides the best value for money. She decides that she wants to now place the order and wishes to speak to a customer service representative directly. Consequently, she logs back on to the Web site and places a call to the customer contact center using the "call me" button. The customer responds to a prompt for the type of inquiry and enters the appropriate selection for sales on the phone. The customer is also prompted for and provides her customer ID number on the phone. The call is routed to an available sales CSR, who accepts the call, receives a CTI-initiated screen pop-up containing contact history information and all previous opportunities logged for the customer in a customized sales view. The customer explains to the CSR that she just created a quote online and wishes to place the quote as an order. The CSR navigates to the quotes screen through the CRM application and locates the quote created by the customer. The CSR is able to confirm the items on the quote, obtains the additional information necessary to convert the quote into an order and transmit the quote to the order fulfillment system to generate an order number.

Has performance driven CRM been created? Not yet. The CPP must be created for this customer. The customer information and preferences must be now logged into a newly created customer file. This customer is Web savvy, and, therefore, it may be beneficial to periodically send Web offers to this customer based on her current computer configuration and needs.

The QSPP must also be given appropriate consideration. The Web interaction and following contact center conversation is combined in a single file and reviewed by the CSR supervisor? Was accurate and complete information provided on the web? Should Web pages be updated? Was sufficient clarification provide? Did the CSR miss any sales opportunities?

As in the previous example, this scenario shows us the following:

- the importance of the CPP, but in this case, the particular customer preferences and needs

- critical tools to enable the CPP—IVR, CTI and CRM applications, including Web-enabling tools

- the need for a QSPP to ensure that quality service is provided to the customer

CASE STUDY 3

Reaching Out—
e-Mail Auto and Suggested Response

In the case that follows, we walk through another example that shows the necessary integration of the multichannel contact center. An organization cannot assume that self-help receives support from the contact center when the customer requests this. And the customer requires you to recognize where help is required and to offer this up willingly, accurately and supportively. To achieve performance driven CRM, these channels (telephone, Internet, face-to-face, mobile communication and more) must coexist and support one another. Regardless of the channel in use by the customer, the customer warrants the same level of service—a high-value customer in one channel, the Internet, must be recognized as having similar values when chatting with a company over the phone or through Web chat. It is only by coordinating and synergizing the CPP and QSPP that this can be accomplished. Here's our last scenario.

A customer browses the Web site looking for product information, but unable to locate what she needs, initiates an inquiry via the structured e-mail option provided on the Web site. After entering the required information on the e-mail including the customer ID and appropriate subject for the inquiry, the customer sends the e-mail which is routed to an available sales CSR. An automatic response is sent back to the customer, acknowledging receipt of the e-mail. The sales CSR responds to the e-mail by inserting a suggested response generated by the system based on the e-mail content into the e-mail response (e.g., if the key words in the message are hard drive and size options, then a e-mail automatic response will provide a message showing the size options, criteria for choice and pricing options).

The customer receives the e-mail, opens the URL link to the product detail information included in the e-mail response and browses through the product content information. She wishes to contact the customer contact center to ask about product comparison information, so she uses the "talk to us live" button in order to contact the customer contact center. She selects the desired format for the interaction—Web call back, voice-over IP (VOIP) or Web chat. The call request is routed to the appropriate CSR, who is alerted to the type of interaction that is being initiated based on the customer's selection. The CSR accepts the call and receives a screen pop-up containing contact history for the customer. Once connected with the CSR using one of the above formats, the customer explains that she would like to view comparison information on two product models. The sales CSR looks up the two product models and pushes product detail pages on each to the customer's desktop. The customer is able to view the product details for each of the two product models side by side. The CSR agent then pushes an order form to the customer to complete and retrieves it from the customer to review for completeness. Once it is complete, the CSR agent pushes the completed form back to the customer for submission.

This scenario has a strong focus on the QSPP, but as you can see there are a number of CPP issues that are addressed as well. The example shows us the following:

- the care and attention to quality service issues, accuracy and completeness of information
- heavy reliance on self-help features and self-validation as well as CTI, Web chat tools, push technology and CRM suite functionality
- where a CPP can enhance the customer experience and customer recognition so that a degree of personalization can occur

CHECKLIST—WHAT DID WE LEARN?

For each case, we have checked off the appropriate boxes to indicate the multichannel capabilities highlighted in the case, key performance driven CRM performance program components, technology requirements and potential benefits to be achieved with this capability. What other CPP and QSPP issues can you identify?

	Case 1	Case 2	Case 3
Demonstrated Capability			
Real-time integration of customer interactions across sales channels (Internet and customer contact center)		x	
Video chat		x	
VoIP, Web call back, Web chat			x
Back-office integration		x	
Capture of customer-entered data	x		
Skills-based routing based on service requested	x		x
Audio response e-mail			x
Web collaboration			x
Use of captured data to enable screen pop-up of correct screen for service with customer details	x		
Form sharing			x
Knowledge management	x		
Cross-sell of campaign populated through relationship marketing	x		
Smart scripting	x		
Customer segmentation			
Campaign planning and execution			

	Case 1	Case 2	Case 3
Performance Program Requirement			
Understand customer	X	X	X
Understand organization		X	X
Commitment to QSPP	X	X	X
Technology/Tool Enabler Required			
CTI	X	X	X
Data mining	X		
Campaign management tool	X		
Web content	X		X
Value modelling	X	X	
CSR CRM workbench	X	X	X
CRM database	X	X	X
Tiered service	X	X	X
Video chat		X	
Potential Business Benefits Achievable			
Intelligent routing to the most appropriate agent maximizes customer satisfaction by minimizing handoffs.	X	X	X
Minimal handoffs deliver internal efficiency savings, help increase customer contact center capacity and reduce costs.	X	X	X
Screen pops-ups reduce call handling times and therefore cost. Secondary benefits include minimizing data duplication and fragmenttion of customer records.	X	X	X
Content management enables sharing of information and eliminates data duplication.	X	X	
Customer segmentation facilitates customer value routing and determines level of customer service (customer who is of higher value to the organization is routed to a more specialized CSR).	X		

	Case 1	Case 2	Case 3
Customer segmentation enables target marketing (cross-sell, upsell).	x		
Smart scripting ensures consistency of customer service delivery.	x		
Content management enables sharing of information and eliminates data duplication.	x		
Company Web site enables customer self-service, allowing customer activity through an additional communication channel.		x	x
Web site reduces requirement for customer service to perform basic transactions (i.e., researching company product information, creating order to purchase products).		x	x
The transaction cost for the activity is very low.			x
Web e-mail structure enables routing based on customer-entered data.			x
It enables real-time form collaboration.			x
Online configuration ensures accurate order entry.		x	
It enables real-time integration with back office systems.		x	
Web e-mail structure enables automated response acknowledging receipt of e-mail.			x
Sales cycle time is reduced.	x	x	x

SUMMARY

To achieve performance driven CRM, leading organizations have recognized that there is no single channel that can provide lasting customer satisfaction. Rather, a multichannel contact center approach is required. Remember that whatever the nature or point of contact, customers want a seamless interaction throughout their experience with the company. Companies that succeed in doing this reap enormous benefits—as does everyone who conducts business with them.

A strong Customer Performance Program is crucial. But it must work hand in hand with the Quality Service Performance Program. And both must be supported with the proper mix of technology to enable these programs, regardless of the preferred channel of interaction. Both must be fed with new information, sorted and resorted to ensure that value is added to the customer experience.

Staying the Course—
Focusing on Your People

Developing the three performance programs gives you the full range of enablers for performance driven CRM. However, progressive and leading organizations understand and embrace that in order to be successful, performance driven CRM must involve your employees. Involvement means the following:

- Give your employees CRM vision direction that they can all see and understand. Make it real for them through clearly articulated expectations and targets that are part of the CRM vision.

- Demonstrate to employees through performance coaching and reward programs what each individual does that contributes to success.

Bringing employees to their full potential means bringing the organization to its full potential, which, in turn, means being in a position to realize your CRM vision. Success is a combination of attitude, performance and behavior. Figure 10-1 demonstrates these three critical requirements for success and the relationship between them. Attitude influences performance and behavior, performance influences behavior and attitude, and behavior influences attitude and performance. Together they achieve success.

Figure 10-1: Three Critical Requirements for Success in PD CRM

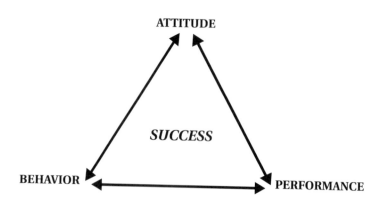

   These organizations understand the importance of *every* employee, and they give each individual a reason for contributing to success. A performance culture is built through a commitment to continuous improvement. Everyone, regardless of position (manager, owner, administrative staff) and status (full-time, part-time or temporary) are part of the performance driven CRM success equation. Simply put, without good employees, you will not be successful at performance driven CRM. Therefore, employees are your most important asset for achieving and staying the CRM course. This is due to the fact that CRM success is achieved through satisfied and high-performing employees who, in turn, create satisfied customers.
   The performance driven CRM balanced scorecard recognizes the importance of employee satisfaction to be equal to operating and financial performance and customer satisfaction. But the bottom line is this: being performance focused on an enterprise-wide CRM basis requires a focus on employees, the need to stimulate employee growth and retain good employees. This is accomplished only one way. Staff must enjoy professional satisfaction, which allows them to achieve personal satisfaction, which cycles back and increases professional satisfaction. All employees are important in this equation. The important factor is not at which level the employees are (e.g., clerical, customer service, managers etc.); it is that all of them are provided with a purpose for contributing to the success of CRM.

What benefits can an organization expect if employee performance is raised?

- better quality service, leading to increased customer service, leading to increased customer satisfaction
- new solutions to old problems through innovation and creativity
- overall lower costs due to lower levels of absenteeism, reduced number of errors and higher productivity
- increased profitability as a result of all the previous points

However, improving and sustaining employee performance is easier said than done. Critical elements for success are commitments to lifelong learning and on-the-job training. In general, performance driven CRM organizations must focus on creating and keeping a bigger talent pool and must create more opportunities and advancement for highly talented people. Organizations that have increased training have achieved higher profits, increased productivity, reduced waste, higher customer satisfaction and retention and a better employee health and safety record. Leading organizations make learning a business strategy by internalizing a learning culture. For example, a learning organization will have a yearly target number of hours for each employee to be dedicated to training/learning. Employees are measured against this target and are rewarded financially if they have met the target. Learning organizations will also dedicate a budget specifically for ongoing employee teaching events, yet only a handful of organizations can truly be called learning organizations.

Organizations are beginning to recognize that innovation breeds success, and innovation is fueled by measuring performance. Measuring employees against how innovative they are sends a clear message that the organization not only supports innovation, but expects it. Innovation requires both investment in enabling resources (such as research, training and technology) and management systems that foster creativity. Research confirms that strong innovators consistently outperform weak innovators. The capacity of organizations to innovate successfully is determined by the quality of their management and leadership. Leaders of highly innovative and performing organizations tend to have the following qualities:

- Customer-oriented and future focused—These organizations ensure (through training, communication, teaching, coaching) that employees are constantly in touch with their customers. Any new product or service developments focus on meeting the next wave of customer expectations.

• Unwavering in their commitment to core values—Organizations that are committed to core values will not sacrifice these values at difficult budget times. If one of the values is to be a learning organization, budget cuts will not take the learning budget away.

• Credible, both internally and externally—Organizations that are credible do good on what they say they are going to do, both for employees and customers.

• Ready for change—These organizations are tenacious but willing to be challenged, to change their minds and to accept that they might be wrong.

• Open to ideas from many sources—All employees are thought of as sources of ideas, as are customers and other leading organizations.

• Committed to organizational learning—These organizations view learning as a necessary part of the job for every employee.

Although the importance of innovation and performance improvement is recognized, organizations often appear to have difficulty in creating the climate, culture, systems and process necessary to generate successful innovation and performance over time. The key to creating this type of climate is to invite employee ownership through a performance improvement journey. Employee ownership occurs when employees take on responsibility for the customer, the relationships required to provide quality service (both internal and external relationships) and their own performance. To create this ownership environment, an organization must individualize the performance improvement journey to each staff member. The outcome of the performance improvement journey is to make employees fit and fast to service customers and exceed in performance. This is done through enhancing core competencies and building new skills.

PERFORMANCE IMPROVEMENT JOURNEY

The journey has four main components:

1. *Beginning the Performance Journey* is the component in which employees must understand what motivates them to improve. Is it for the right reasons? Are they committed to improving?

2. *Planning the Route* is the component during which employees plan their destination. They set the route to improve.

3. *Staying the Course* is the step in which employees make the investment in self and start to take action.

4. *Ensuring Success* is the component in which employees stay focused, adopt a concept of managing upward and practice continuous self-improvement.

Let's take a look back at each of these components.

Beginning the Journey

All of us are enticed by the prospect of taking a journey. Usually, it is not a question of "Do I want to?" but "When do I go?" This should be the same for the performance improvement journey. The question should not be "Do I want to improve my performance?" but "How can I do it?" To determine if your employees should start on a performance improvement journey have them answer the "Yes/No" statements below. If any of the statements are answered with a yes, they are not ready to begin. They are not yet motivated to honestly improve performance for the right reasons. Since considerable effort and resource is required to complete the journey (e.g., money and time), attempting to start the journey now would be a wasted effort for employees, management and the organization. Even if there are existing negative organizational influencers that have forced the employees into answering "yes," they should still not begin the journey since any changes will be only short-term changes.

I feel the need to improve my performance because of the following:

• I want to keep my job.

• I feel my paycheck is tied to improving my performance.

• I want to avoid the pain of confrontation and negative feedback.

• I am feeling peer pressure to improve.

• I know I am being watched and have to improve.

Employees will be ready when their motivation for improving performance shifts from feeling that they *have* to improve performance to *wanting* to improve performance. To determine if they are ready to begin their journey, ask them to answer the following questions honestly:

- Are you prepared to start improving your performance today?
- Given the right tools/environment, can you improve your performance?
- Are there some things you are doing not so well right now?

Assuming that the employees answered the questions honestly, they are ready to start their journey if they have answered "yes" to any of the above questions. Dishonest answers can be uncovered only during the journey. If employees are not progressing through their journey and you have provided them with the required supports, you may want to revisit both sets of questions with them. As your employees start on their performance improvement journey, remind them that they should abide by the following:

> Don't focus on being competitive. If you are attempting to improve performance from a competitive standpoint, you will be continuously trying to catch up. You will be looking behind to see where the competition is rather than looking ahead to see where the next performance improvement level is that you are trying to reach. Improving performance must be about you and your own desire to improve your own quality regardless of where the other person is.

The first step in the performance improvement journey is to make a commitment to be successful. Have employees start by embracing the following list of commitments. Ask them to write a "yes" beside each commitment as they make them. Employees who are fully committed and want to succeed will be able to write a "yes" beside each one. If they cannot, they may not be ready to commit, since all of the committmens listed in the table below are necessary for success.

Table 10-1

Commitment	Make the Commitment
I am ready to improve my performance.	
I will adopt a new performance philosophy, one whereby I will continuously strive to keep improving every day.	
My performance is my responsibility, and I accept that responsibility by taking ownership for my performance.	
Individual goals related to my performance are important to me.	
I have great potential, and I will ensure that I reach it.	
I have good ideas, and I will ensure that I communicate them.	
Improving my performance will increase the pleasure of working.	
I am ready to realize my potential.	
I will embrace quality service even though I know it is a greater effort than ordinary service.	
I will incorporate performance improvement into my daily life and my day-to-day activities.	
I will celebrate my success.	

By making the performance commitment for the right reasons they have begun the commitment process. It is time to kick off their journey and start them thinking about what is affecting their performance and what needs to be improved. The following exercise should be completed by each staff member. This will contribute to the development of their own personal performance plan.

Planning the Route

Now that employees have made the commitment to improving performance, the next stage in the journey is to set the route—to decide what needs improving and where to focus. Determining current employees thinking about where they need to improve performance is the first step. This is accomplished by having employees fill out the questionnaire below: Seven Steps to Kick Off Performance Improvement Thinking. Let employees fill in whatever they feel is appropriate to them. There are no right answers for this questionnaire; it is designed to get employees thinking about where and how they want to improve.

Seven Steps to Kick Off Performance Improvement Thinking

1. If I could change something about the way I perform, I would change my

   _____

   _____

   _____

2. If I could get any training I wanted, it would be

   _____

   _____

   _____

3. If I could do whatever I wanted at work, I would (create your own job description)

   _____

   _____

   _____

4. If I could behave however I wanted to, I would start to

   _____

   _____

   _____

5. The biggest obstacle in improving my current performance is

   _____

   _____

   _____

6. I define a top performer as someone who

_____

_____

_____

7. The two ot three things most affecting my performance are

_____

_____

_____

The next step is to determine current performance levels of employees. To do this, use any performance tools you currently have (e.g., scorecards, employee evaluation forms or assessment forms). If you have no current method of assessing employees, you will have to do this through one-on-one performance discussions with employees and document from your and the employees' perspective how they are currently doing. Once you have done this, you need to determine what employees should continue to do, what they should stop doing and where they need to improve. Organizations find it difficult to determine when employees should stop doing something. Even if something is being done well, it may be that it is no longer required or that it is no longer desired by your customers. These are the activities that employees should stop doing.

> There is nothing more wasteful than doing efficiently
> that which is not necessary.
> —*Samuels Rutgers*

Take a moment to list the things your employees are doing now and are doing well. This list should cover all major functions and responsibilities, but not day-to-day activities. For example, include such things as conduct customer service survey, prepare employee newsletter and participate in team meetings. Do not include such things as arrive at work on time, be in daily attendance unless ill and take appropriate breaks. Now list the corresponding skills and/or characteristics required to complete the functions and responsibilities (e.g., good writing skills and being responsive, creative, reliable and organized). It could be that your employees are well-organized and know how to manage people effectively. Perhaps they are a good team players and are knowledgable in specific areas. Once you have your list of what they are doing well, for each item on the list, ask yourself: Do employees need to keep doing this? Is it still important to the organizations? Is it still important to their roles and customer service? If they need to keep doing the task, can they do it even better? It could be that employees are knowledgeable in an area, but they don't share this knowledge across the organization.

Now list the things that employees are not doing so well. It could be that they are not focused at work, they don't actively listen, they don't plan as well as they should and they are always late on your assignments. Once you have your list of what employees are not doing well ask yourself: Do they need to improve this specific area right now? Can it wait until the next performance improvement journey? Performance improvement journeys usually happen annually. To help create these lists and to determine in more detail what employees should focus on, have employees take the performance diagnostic at the end of this chapter. This diagnostic will also help identify in which areas employees are doing well and in which areas there is potential for improvement.

Staying the Course

In order to stay committed, employees should create their own performance improvement plan (PIP). A PIP is for the individual. Your organization can decide to develop a similar PIP for teams or even for the entire organization. For each area that requires improvement or can be improved, try reversing the situation and complete the following sentence: "If I were performing as I wanted to be in this area, it would look like...." If you are having trouble doing this, try viewing the situation from another person's perspective. For example, how would my customer view this situation and advise me to improve my performance? A PIP should be an easy to follow, step-by-step document that tells you:

- your priority performance improvement area
- how you will measure whether you have improved
- your target of how much and by when you want to improve your performance
- how you will identify and celebrate your success

Start Taking Action

Before employees create their PIPs, here are some easy ways to improve daily performance. Encourage them to implement these quick and easy-to-follow "performance improvement rules" and you will see an immediate impact. In any activities they do, have them behave as if it was all up to them, be involved, go the extra mile, double-check the work, smile, care and have fun. Employees who implement these immediately improve their attitude, behavior and performance.

Pretend it is all up to you!
This helps you keep your focus.

Get involved and stay involved.
This helps you complete the job fully.

Always try to do something a little "extra."
This helps put you in front and get noticed.

Always do a double-check.
This helps you ensure quality.

Smile.
This helps to "brighten" your attitude.

Care.
This helps to ensure you give the right amount of attention.

Have fun!
This helps to ensure you stay committed.

Now it is time for your employees to draft their PIPs. Follow the steps, and use the templates provided in Appendix B.

One last word of advice. When setting targets stretch a little. Don't make the goal so easy to reach that you can get there too fast. You will get bored. Your targets should look almost impossible the first time you read them back to yourself.

> Four short words sum up what has lifted most
> successful individuals above the crowd: a little bit more.
> They did all that was expected of them and a little bit more.
>   —*A. Lou Vickery*

Ensuring Success

Now that your employees have prepared their PIPs they will need coaching and assistance staying focused. Most organizations have direct managers as coaches. More progressive organizations have trained senior employees who act as objective coaches. If done right at the beginning of the performance improvement journey, employees will be excited, committed and motivated. This assumes that the organization has introduced the journey in a positive, supportive manner. Employees have been advised that taking this journey is a critical step in achieving performance driven CRM and delighting your customers. However, all too often, a performance improvement journey is either viewed negatively or put to the side and is forgotten before any improvments are made. This is a result of the organization having too little focus on the PIP and so making it unimportant to employees, not tying the actual completion and follow-up of the PIP to compensation and not having the appropriate coaches in place.

To help demonstrate to employees the improtance of the PIP and to help them stay focused the organization should draft a performance improvement mission statement, which will help employees understand the priority for improvement. Employees can then create their own performance improvement mission statement that they can read over each time their interest wavers or every week that passes without taking action on their PIPs. One of the best ways to develop your mission statement is to conduct employee focus groups and ask employees what would demonstrate that the PIP is an important component of performance driven CRM. Below is an example of performance improvement mission statements for the organization that you may want to model yours after or at least kick-start your employees focus groups with. Details describing exactly what each statement means to your specific organization should be developed, include such things as:

* How will you solicit feedback and how often?

* What is the process for providing feedback?

* How will the level of support and encouragment be measured?

Our organization commits to improving our employee's performance, and by doing so, we will do the following:

- Solicit feedback about the tools and support required for our employees to be successful.
- Provide feedback on employee performance on a monthly basis in a supportive and encouraging manner.
- Ensure planned improvements are customer-focused.
- Assist employees to get faster and better by providing the right tools and training.
- Be passionate about the performance improvement journey.
- Maximize people and technology.
- Be flexible.
- Strive to create excellence.
- Nurture employee spirit through performance recognition.
- Be creative and innovative, and encourage creativity and innovation.
- Continue to be performance-focused, and take performance improvement action.

The following is an example of an individual performance improvement statement that aligns with the organizational one above.

I commit to improving my performance, and by doing so I will do the following:

- Solicit feedback about my performance on a monthly basis from my peers and supervisor.
- Be customer-focused.
- Get faster and better.
- Be passionate about learning and performing better.
- Maximize people around me and technology.
- Be flexible.
- Strive to improve continuosly my performance with my customers.
- Nurture my spirit through self-recognition around my performance.
- Be creative and innovative.
- Continue to take performance improvement action.

To further ensure the commitment to performance improvement in your organization, you should consider introducing a structured program that includes a standardized process for providing employees coaching and support and also introduces the concept of an employee performance agreement. Typically, this type of agreement lists the role and responsibilities of employees and the expected behaviour the organization requires from employees, and it also incorporates an employee's PIP. The document acts as a formal agreement between the organization and individual staff member. See Chapter 8 for a sample of an employee performance agreement.

Providing Rewards

Employee should want to do more and be better. Successful organizations understand the impact of motivating employees and providing positive feedback as well as the value of reward-based performance systems. Understanding this, it is important to build a rewards-based system that encompasses many different types of rewards for various achievements. However, rewards are not rewards unless they are recognized as such by employees. For example, even the best, most expensive sporting event seats are wasted on employees who are not sports fans. Nonmonetary rewards should be designed with employee input to ensure that employees will view these as actual rewards with value. You should give employees a nonmonetary reward simply because you believe they would want it. Another coffee cup with the company logo may not be something that they consider a reward. The easiest reward is the compensation reward, but look for other rewards that are either nonmonetary or have cash value. The following is a list of rewards that have worked in high-performing organizations. But remember, when giving rewards, individualize them as much as possible. For example:

- give greater authority
- demonstrate additional trust
- provide written or verbal recognition
- rotate assignments to coveted special projects
- provide stock options
- allow profit sharing
- provide performance bonuses
- issue achievement awards

- allow sabbaticals for long-term employees
- be competitive in pay structures
- demonstrate respect
- increase management access
- develop creative financial rewards (e.g., teams are paid bonuses)

CREATING THE RIGHT ENVIRONMENT

Your employees will engage in the performance improvement journey only if you have created the right environment to ensure maximum benefit from your people. You must build a smooth terrain for employees. Eliminate the barriers to performance as much as possible. For example, eliminate unnecessary approvals or unhealthy work environments. The environment has to shift from one in which top management directs, controls and instructs employees to an environment in which employees participate, are proactive and are influenced and encouraged to align with the overall CRM vision. You are moving from a top-down to a bottom-up environment. This shift is essential to ensure that the organization is fit and ready to achieve the CRM vision and to enable employees to be at their best. Figure 10-2 on the following page demonstrates the shift required in the management environment to achieve performance driven CRM success.

SUMMARY

The following five critical success factors discussed in this chapter are summarize in Table 10-2 on the following page as to what an organization (management and the coaches) is required to do to ensure employees perform at optimal levels. Take the test, and see if your organization measures up.

If followed correctly, performance driven CRM should alter your employee's attitudes (remember we mean *all* employees, regardless of position and level). The left side of Figure 10-3 below lists employee attitude in an organization without performance driven CRM. Compare this to the right side in an organization in which performance driven CRM and a focus on employees have been successfully implemented.

Figure 10-2: The Shift Neccessary to Achieving the PD CRM Vision

A SHIFT:

From a Reactive Output Management Environment	To a Proactive Outcome Management Environment
Designed to:	**Designed to:**
• control employee efforts	• create employee value and input
• police compliance with rules	• motivage, energize, align efforts
• document past performance scores	• enable enhanced performance
Focused on:	**Focused on:**
• history—"how did we do?"	• the future—"how can we improve?"
• input and output targets	• outcomes for people, customers, stakeholders
• reactive short-term solutions	• opportunities leading to long-term success
• symptoms of problems	• drivers of success
Feels:	**Feels:**
• static, boring, restrictive	• creative, mobilized, active
• critical, stifling	• supportive, encouraging
• negative, gray, cold	• positive, inviting, warm

Table 10-2 Five Critical Success Factors to Ensure High Levels of Performance

1. Have you given your staff members a direction they can all see? Have you made it real for them through expectations, targets and stretch targets? Have you demonstrated what each individual does that contributes most?

2. Have you given each individual a reason for contributing to performance driven CRM success? Have you built a performance culture through a commitment to continuous improvement?

3. Have you made employees fit and fast? Have you determined required core competencies, training and enablers?

4. Have you made employees want to do more and be better? Have you done this through a proactive measurement program based on rewards and recognition?

5. Have you built a smooth terrain for employees. Have you done this through positive measurement?

Figure 10-3: Staff Attitudes With and Without PD CRM

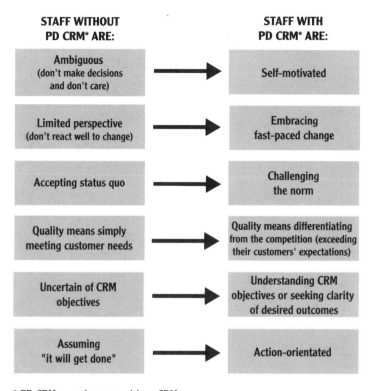

STAFF WITHOUT PD CRM* ARE:		STAFF WITH PD CRM* ARE:
Ambiguous (don't make decisions and don't care)	→	Self-motivated
Limited perspective (don't react well to change)	→	Embracing fast-paced change
Accepting status quo	→	Challenging the norm
Quality means simply meeting customer needs	→	Quality means differentiating from the competition (exceeding their customers' expectations)
Uncertain of CRM objectives	→	Understanding CRM objectives or seeking clarity of desired outcomes
Assuming "it will get done"	→	Action-orientated

* PD CRM = performance driven CRM

CHECKLIST—THE PERFORMANCE DIAGNOSTIC: Characteristics of a High Performer

Do you think you are a high performer? Try the following self-test to see where your strengths and weaknesses are and whether or not you feel you can improve your performance. Select only one box per characteristic. *Be honest with yourself.*
Good Luck!

I am…

	Yes ☺	No ☹	I can do better ✓
Accessible	❏	❏	❏
Communicative	❏	❏	❏
Mature	❏	❏	❏
Sincere	❏	❏	❏
Proactive	❏	❏	❏
Responsive	❏	❏	❏
Self-motivated	❏	❏	❏
Innovative	❏	❏	❏
Creative	❏	❏	❏
Reliable	❏	❏	❏
Effective	❏	❏	❏
Efficient	❏	❏	❏
Knowledgeable	❏	❏	❏
A team player	❏	❏	❏
Respectful	❏	❏	❏
Goal-oriented	❏	❏	❏
Quality-oriented	❏	❏	❏

I am...

	Yes ☺	No ☹	I can do better ✓
Committed	❏	❏	❏
A problem solver	❏	❏	❏
Tolerant of others	❏	❏	❏
Honest	❏	❏	❏
Organized	❏	❏	❏
Always learning	❏	❏	❏
Nonconfrontational	❏	❏	❏
Receptive to change	❏	❏	❏
Open-minded	❏	❏	❏
Self-confident	❏	❏	❏
Diplomatic	❏	❏	❏
Appropriately friendly	❏	❏	❏

I do...

	Yes	No	I can do better
Provide positive/constructive feedback	❏	❏	❏
Seek and encourage participation	❏	❏	❏
Use common sense	❏	❏	❏
Lead by example	❏	❏	❏

I do...	Yes ☺	No ☹	I can do better ✓
Show initiative	❏	❏	❏
Have a professional attitude	❏	❏	❏
Exercise good judgment	❏	❏	❏
Listen	❏	❏	❏
Live company values	❏	❏	❏
Demonstrate flexibility	❏	❏	❏
Think conceptually	❏	❏	❏
Inspire others	❏	❏	❏
Have strong self-esteem	❏	❏	❏
Act as a mentor to others	❏	❏	❏
Influence others positively	❏	❏	❏
Have good interpersonal skills	❏	❏	❏
Plan well	❏	❏	❏
Have good writing skills	❏	❏	❏
Have good presentation skills	❏	❏	❏
Have good coaching skills	❏	❏	❏
Manages stress	❏	❏	❏
Take calculated risks	❏	❏	❏

Congratulations! One of the most difficult things to do is to assess your own performance *honestly*. The next step is to analyze your self-test and see just how high of a performer you really are! (You won't need a calculator for this.)

Give yourself five points for each ✓ =   _____

Give yourself three points for each ☺ =   _____

Give yourself one points for each ☹ =   _____

Now, add up the points and enter the total in the "performance box" below.

One of the main reasons that you get more points for each "I can do better" (✓) and "I do not" is because only high performers can see the value in admitting that they may need improvement.

You can ALWAYS improve your performance.

Realizing that your performance may need a "tune up" actually indicates that you are on your way to becoming a higher performer than you are now.

- If you scored between **200 and 255**, you are a high performer and realize that improvement leads to success not only in your career, but in your personal life as well. Keep up the good work!

- If you scored between **52 and 199**, you are performing well in certain areas and feel that you can increase your performance in others. However, there are certain critical areas in which you may feel that you cannot improve. We would recommend that you write these down to prove to yourself why you cannot "do better."

Ask yourself these three questions:

- Am I being honest with myself?

- Am I afraid to improve in this area or feel that I am not being encouraged enough?

- Do I lack the skills to improve this performance?

If you answered "yes" to even one of these questions, it is your responsibility to seek the appropriate assistance and coaching to not only improve your performance, but to build your self-confidence in your current abilities.

- If you scored between **51 or less**, you do not believe there are any areas that you could do better in. We would recommend that you review the diagnostic again, and think about what you could do better in over the next month. Ask yourself why you cannot do better in any areas.

Ask yourself these three questions:

- Am I being honest with myself?

- Am I afraid to improve in this area or feel that I am not being encouraged enough?

- Do I lack the skills to improve this performance?

If you answered "yes" to even one of these questions, it is your responsibility to seek the appropriate assistance and coaching to not only improve your performance, but to build your self-confidence in your current abilities.

> "The great thing in this world is not so much
> where we are but in what direction we are moving."
> —*Oliver Wendell Holmes*

Conclusion—How to Ensure that Performance Driven CRM Becomes a Reality:

WATCH OUT FOR THESE PITFALLS

What is the best way to end a book? Perhaps it is with some lessons learned from those that failed and a reference back to previous chapters of the book to offer up solutions. Whether your organization is about to embark on a new initiative to deliver performance driven CRM or it requires a bit of fine-tuning, we think that you will find the following an effective guide. Successful organizations understand that innovation comes from what works for others. Accordingly, these companies constantly review the best practices of others and adopt those that suit their needs. So we invite you to do the same.

What follows are some tips to ensure that your performance driven CRM initiative does not fail. The issues are not unique to any one industry or size of company, but there is one common thread: to be successful, you must focus on standards, measurement and facts, and that is why performance driven CRM is absolutely critical.

Reviewing the success stories of those organizations that have well-regarded performance driven CRM initiatives suggest the following five broad categories in identifying why traditional CRM initiatives may fail:

1. Management Commitment
   a) lack of strong visible management commitment

2. Inadequate Business Case

   a) insufficient attention to the right issues and questions

   b) focusing on revenue enhancement or cost reduction only, rather than the true costs and benefits

   c) poor definition of human and financial resources

3. Lack of Performance Standards

   a) a reluctance to establish standards of performance and measure against them

4. CRM Culture not Encouraged

   a) insufficient continuous communication

   b) resistance to change

5. Inadequate Transition Planning

   a) a poorly defined coordinating and action-oriented structure

   b) taking on too much, too soon

No book would be complete without some additional discussion of each of these five items. Even if you think you have heard it all before, please continue to read on. Our perspective may be somewhat different from others.

MANAGEMENT COMMITMENT

Performance driven CRM cannot be implemented as a bottom-up initiative. It must be driven from the most senior levels, and visible executive sponsorship must be provided. Unless senior management is committed, it will not get attention, focus or budget. It will be short lived and be considered someone else's initiative. With no senior level ownership, there is no impetus and no burning platform. And one more issue. It must be an enterprise-wide initiative. It cannot be relegated to a single department or division—it must be enterprise-wide and backed with sufficient visible and monetary support.

Lack of Strong Visible Management Commitment

Senior management commitment to the initiative is critical not only for the purpose of initially embracing a performance improvement process, but also in sustaining it. Management must drive the initiative. Having established a commitment, it must reinforce it visibly throughout the entire organization, possibly through its direct involvement in the initiative, by keeping this as an agenda item at management meetings, through president's letters to staff or even town hall meetings.

Experience shows that securing sponsorship is time-consuming, but it is fundamental to the success of any performance driven CRM initiative. Recognize that this initiative will take a minimum of 18 months to realize true long-term benefits. Without long-term management support, interest will wane. Allow for sufficient time to secure real sponsorship, and check that all sponsors have bought into the following:

- The baseline situation—This means, what is the current "as-is" situation, current performance and operating practices and the need for change—the "burning platform?"

- The cost/benefit case—How much will need to be invested in process redesign, technology, implementation and change management? How long will it take to realize the benefits over and above this investment, on both a quantitative and qualitative basis?

- The means of realizing the benefits—What type of investment or change in culture will be required? This may include the role of senior management, the impact on staff, and even compensation and incentive adjustments.

- Their role in making it happen—They will have to do more than talk about how important this initiative is. They will have to be active participants and show a willingness to change since it may require a new operating structure. Titles and responsibilities may also change.

CFOs play an important role here, too. They must be involved in tracking investments in far-flung parts of the enterprise and consolidating them to build muscle in vendor negotiations.

Reference: Chapter 1

INADEQUATE BUSINESS CASE

Typically, senior executives ask: What is this going to cost me, and when will I see the benefits? The answer to this question comes from a realization of where you are today and how far you need to go to see the initial impact of performance driven CRM. What are the priorities, what are the new competencies that are required, and how quickly must this be implemented? Are you focusing on the right questions and issues? Read on.

Insufficient Attention to the Right Issues and Questions

Performance driven CRM is not easy because it is not just about increasing revenue or reducing costs. And it will not get any easier if you do not focus on the right questions. These questions must address your current competencies in understanding, managing, anticipating and personalizing the customer experience—where are you now, and where do you need to be?

And that means addressing the following four strategies:

1. Customer Strategy

2. Product and Channel Strategy

3. Infrastructure Strategy

4. Performance Management Strategy

Each of these must be articulated with sufficient clarity so that management can understand and commit the needed human and physical resources. What questions must be addressed in each area to implement such a strategy effectively? Consider each strategy.

Customer Strategy

Your customer strategy must be an articulation based on facts, not passion, of what degree of differentiation you are prepared to give your customer base. Ask yourself the following questions:

• What are your key customer segments, based on current and future customer needs?

• Are there distinct customer segments that have unique needs?

• Are there certain customer segments that should be offered unique products and services?

• Do you have unique approaches in place to ensure customer loyalty and retention?

• Have you established a win-win relationship with the customer?

Product and Channel Strategy

Once you have a customer strategy, the next question that has to be addressed is: Which products will I offer to which customer segments, through which channels and where or to which customers am I prepared to offer differentiated service? Consider the following questions:

- Do customers prefer to receive the products or services through a particular channel of distribution such as the Internet, fax, mail, or telephone?
- What are the preferred channels through which to interface with the customer from an organizational perspective?
- What are the costs per channel?
- Which products and services should be directed through which channels to the which customer segments?
- What channel conflicts can possibly occur, and how do you plan to address them?

Infrastructure Strategy

Technology and people are the enablers of any customer strategy. Unfortunately, most organizations lean too heavily on technology and confuse that with the overall CRM strategy. Consider the following: Your situation is the result of your lack of responsiveness and focus on the customer. Technology alone is not the solution if your processes that touch your customers do not change. You have to become a business that is easy to do business with. But more than that, you have to change the way you do business internally—the organizational infrastructure—and that will require a new enterprise-wide structure and realignment of departments. Ask yourself these questions:

- What common technology infrastructure is required?
- What technology will be required to create a learning organization?
- What new CRM practices, processes and tools are required?
- What new organizational and people competencies are needed in order to implement the CRM strategy successfully?

Performance Management Strategy

To create lasting CRM, there must be a performance driven component. To quote Peter Drucker, "What does not get measured, does not get done." The performance programs are the heart and soul of this strategy, and the questions that must be asked include:

- What information is needed for continuous improvement?

- Do we have a balanced view of the issues (customer satisfaction, employee satisfaction, operating performance, stakeholder needs)?

- Are we measuring with the right frequency and obtaining sufficient information to make change?

- Are new feedback mechanisms required, and is the organization aligned to take action?

Once these questions are addressed, a set of synergies may emerge.

Reference: Chapters 1, 2, 3 and 6

Focusing on Revenue Enhancement or Cost Reduction Only, Rather than the True Costs and Benefits

Too often, companies take the path of least resistance. They find it too easy to cut costs because the benefits seem obvious. But sometimes, you have to spend money to make money even if it is more difficult to justify revenue benefits. Those that have been most successful have focused on both costs and revenues. But in order to calculate benefits, a baseline of the current situation is needed as a means of comparison. The baseline should identify the current situation against which benefits will be monitored. As improvements will be measured by referencing against this baseline (and this is the key to success for performance driven CRM), it is essential that the baseline case against which benefits are compared has full sponsorship across the business. Otherwise benefits will not be credible.

Then, the costs of the CRM program needs to be fully outlined, making it clear which costs need approval. Costs of a performance driven CRM program will vary dramatically depending on the type and scale of the program—the more people that will need access to information, the regional diversity in existence, the speed of change required and more will affect costs to implement. In our experience, we have found that there are at least 12 factors that will affect the investment required to achieve the required benefits. Some are more substantial than others, but all are relevant. They include the following:

- The number of users involved—The more users, obviously, the higher the costs. But how many are required initially, and how many more over time?
- The number of geographical locations.
- The number of functions involved—Is just contact management required, or will campaign management, complaint tracking, dispatching or other functions be required, and when?
- The extent of process reengineering required.
- The amount of systems configuration required—How many and what types of legacy systems will have to be interfaced?
- The extent of integration needed with back-office systems such as enterprise resource planning (ERP).
- Whether new hardware is required.
- Whether an existing office systems/communications infrastructure is in place.
- Whether other relevant change management initiatives are already in progress—Don't ignore the need for, and the extent of, change management required. Employee resistance will spell disaster.
- Availability of good in-house resources.
- Quality and accessibility of existing data.[1]

While cost accuracy is important, don't spend too much time getting it down to the closest decimal point. Experience shows that sensitivity of the costs of a CRM program tends to be +/- 10 percent. However, benefits, particularly when revenue-oriented, can vary by +/- 200 percent. This means that greater emphasis should be given to ensuring benefits are realistic rather than ensuring exact accuracy of costings.

And don't forget the true benefits. Benefit cases are likely to contain multiple benefits. There are three types that you must address:

1. Revenue Benefits

2. Cost Reductions

3. Quantitative and Qualitative Benefits

---

[1] Hewson Consulting Group, February 2000.

Revenue Benefits

Where will revenue increase, by how much, and by when? Revenue benefits used to justify CRM business cases typically are as follows:

- acquisition increases (e.g., by reducing the acquisition cycle time, or the time, and investment required to acquire a new customer)

- increased cross-selling (e.g., by improving success rates from attempts to cross-sell)

- increased upselling (e.g., by moving customers onto higher specification products)

- customer retention improvements (e.g., delivering improved customer service and thus, holding onto customers longer)

- product mix improvements (e.g., by selling a greater proportion of higher margin products)

- customer mix improvements (e.g., by selling more to customers who buy more or higher margin products)

- price protection/increases (e.g., by increasing service levels, which can add value and therefore lead to price defense, price increases or reduced price sensitivity)

Cost Reductions

Where are the opportunities to reduce unnecessary work, such as redundancies, double-entering of data and other wasted efforts. Cost reduction benefits that are commonly used to justify CRM business cases include the following:

- reduced customer contact management costs (e.g., telephone contact reducing the number of direct calls required)

- improved marketing/sales effectiveness (e.g., reduced direct mail costs through better targeting or personalization)

- reduced labor costs due to automated processes (e.g., automated call routing and basic call answering in a call center)

- lower staff turnover due to improved motivation, thereby reducing recruitment and training costs

- reduced system development and support costs from replacing legacy systems (it may be less costly to replace systems than to upgrade and maintain old ones)
- reduced inventory costs due to better sales forecasting

Quantitative and Qualitative Benefits

These benefits come in the form of improved customer satisfaction, improved operating performance and efficiencies. These improvement metrics should be clear and measurable. Examples might be:

- percent improvement in conversion rate for new customers
- percent increase in customer lifetime value
- percent increase in average sales per customer
- percent improvement in customer response rates to marketing activity

Any secondary benefits should also be identified and outlined. For instance, secondary benefits might include decreased stock levels, less obsolescence etc.

Fundamentally, lasting CRM—performance driven CRM—is about managing the enterprise around customer interactions and therefore maximizing the value of customer relationships. Therefore, revenue benefits should ultimately be driven off multiple metrics, the ultimate ones being those that measure an organization's success in developing customer relationships. To identify possible metrics, the following questions should be explored:

- What proportion of your potential target customers do you currently have? How many could you have?
- What is the current value of these relationships? What is the potential value of these relationships?
- How long on average do your customers remain with the company? What if they stayed longer?
- Who are the best customers? What is their value to you, and how can you increase that?
- What would happen to the value of different customer segments if the product changed?

Reference: Chapters 1, 3 and 9

Poor Definition of Required Human and Financial Resources

A CRM initiative must have adequate resources dedicated to it if it is to succeed. These resources include people and their time, financial resources and technology. Many organizations find it quite difficult to quantify the costs of their program. The problems associated with measuring people's time and the value of that time is the primary reason for this. Literature suggests that a quality/customer satisfaction initiative can take up to 15 percent of an employee's normal working hours plus additional time for supplementary training, and it can require much more in certain areas of management or other specific employees.

Work overload and lack of time are cited as major factors affecting CRM success. CRM initiatives are intended to improve quality and productivity, but the staff can't find the time to implement the initiative properly. Similarly, adequate financial resources and investment in technology must be provided to support the initiative.

Reference: Chapters 2, 5 and 8

LACK OF PERFORMANCE STANDARDS

While we have spoken about this time and time again, it deserves special mention once again. Performance driven CRM will not occur if there is no dedication and commitment to continuous improvement. Measurement is therefore critical, and measurement without standards and a learning environment is senseless.

A Reluctance to Establish Standards of Performance

Organizations that have successfully embraced performance driven CRM recognize the importance of standards/measures and the need to constantly measure performance in order to achieve lasting customer relationship management. That is why it is essential that performance be compared against established standards because, otherwise, all of the words and pronouncements about customer satisfaction and quality customer care quickly become hollow. When people find that they are actually accountable for performance improvement in customer satisfaction, they are motivated to ensure that improvement. A real sense of the organization's commitment is established through actions. Within successful organizations, performance improvement initiatives are designed and implemented to achieve clearly defined goals or objectives.

CASE STUDY
Xerox and Exxon

At Xerox, a recognized leader in quality customer care, measures are incorporated into individual and group performance evaluations and are part of the basis for rewards and compensation. The goals are set in two ways: bottom-up and the top-down. Xerox is more of a top-down advocate. Within this organization, top management sets company-wide goals which cascade down throughout the organization. The sum total of all the goals of each division is the overall goal established by senior management in the first place. Each division clearly understands the role it must play in the establishment of the total corporate goal.

The bottom-up approach is one popularized by Exxon. Within this organization, process teams at lower levels of the organization set their own goals in a coordinated and controlled manner, resulting in a synergy to improve overall company performance.

Provided that there is top management commitment and buy-in, either approach will work.

Reference: Chapters 3, 4, 5 and 10

CRM CULTURE NOT ENCOURAGED

There is a golden rule of service that is used by leading organizations: "Do unto your employees, as you would have them do unto your customers." If the employee base is not committed to quality service and does not eat sleep and breath quality service, it is unlikely that your customers will receive this. Some organizations are almost fanatic about this; it is almost a religion, a cult. Regardless, it is a culture that must be adopted by the whole organization.

Insufficient Continuous Communication

Once senior management commits to the process, the goals and progress toward those goals must be continuously communicated to staff at all levels of the organization so that everyone in the organization shares the vision. An important binding element of successful initiatives is employee buy-in and participation. To achieve this, the entire employee base must believe that senior management is committed to the program. This can be conveyed either through actions or words, but as the saying goes, action speaks louder.

Communication must be ongoing throughout the course of the initiative. It maintains awareness and supports the process of continuous improvement. By continuing to publish newsletters, celebrate success and generally convey the CRM/customer service message, employees will come to believe that the program is not a fad and is an inherent component of their everyday activities. Communication activities can include the establishment of CRM weeks, a monthly newsletter, bimonthly CRM award ceremonies, and more, to continue to keep CRM and customer service at the forefront.

Reference: Chapters 7 and 10

Resistance to Change

Previously established paradigms and resistance to change can severely handicap an initiative. Machiavelli put it well:

It must be remembered that there is nothing more difficult to plan, more doubtful to succeed, nor more dangerous to manage than the creation of a new system. For the initiator has the enmity of all who would profit by the preservation of the old institution and merely lukewarm defenders in those who would gain by the new one.

It is often difficult to change the preformed and accepted mindsets people have of the way work should be conducted. Some see this as a challenge to their competency; others are just plain cynical and will resist anything that is new or that will impact what they currently do. After all, they have seen or read about other initiatives, in other companies, or even in their own, that have failed. Why should it be different this time?

In order to succeed, you will probably have to cheat the system— pilot projects that can succeed within a 90-day time frame, projects that demonstrate the benefits that can be achieved. Success breeds success. When managers see the benefits and high likelihood of success, they will commit and support the initiative.

Reference: Chapter 10

INADEQUATE TRANSITION PLANNING

A Poorly Defined Coordinating and Action-Oriented Structure

The infrastructure used to coordinate and implement the performance improvement initiative can also be critical to its success. Organizations with successful initiatives advocate a structure that is harmonious with the existing organizational structure. Cross-functional teams or councils appear to be the most successful. Critical considerations include the following questions:

- How many initiatives and changes in process and practices must occur?

- How should they be staged to maximize and realize benefits quickly?

- What technology enablers must be implemented, and what are the priorities for implementation?

- What team composition is required to ensure focus? What responsibilities and accountabilities will they be assigned?

At GM, natural teams are formed around processes and include a diagonal as well as cross-functional membership, so several disciplines and levels of management and different functions are involved. But care must to taken to educate and support these teams properly. Inadequate and insufficient training are also common causes of failure or, at best, limited success in CRM initiatives. Having committed to and bought into the initiative, people must understand their roles and have the skills and knowledge to fill these functions. They must have the tools and training to implement the program successfully.

Our research and experience suggests that with organizations that have successfully implemented performance driven CRM, over 85 percent have implemented quality/customer service training programs, and over 90 percent of those organizations state that that training was an effective part of their initiative.

Reference: Chapters 1, 2, 9 and 10

Taking On Too Much, Too Soon

Splitting large CRM programs into a number of individual, smaller projects simplifies complexity. Some organizations break the implementation down into a series of 90-day initiatives, each with practical deliverables and measurable benefits. For complex programs, dividing the implementation into a number of individual projects has the following benefits:

• It aids understanding of the program across the business.

• It enables individual parts of the program to be prioritized and scheduled accordingly.

• It enables sponsorship to be sought for each project in turn. In fact, a sponsor should be identified for each individual project. This person should take ownership of the project benefits, ensuring they are realized and monitoring achievement.

When a program is broken down into a series of projects, it is important to do the following:

• Clearly identify any benefits that pertain to the entire program in aggregate. The benefits will not be realized if all parts of the program are not implemented.

• Identify clear standards for prioritizing individual projects. These criteria might include financial impact, degree of implementation difficulty, relative impact on customer satisfaction or alignment with business strategy.

Reference: Chapters 5 and 8

CHECKLIST—THINGS TO REMEMBER AS YOU START OFF ON YOUR JOURNEY

Earlier, we spoke about the common pitfalls or traps to avoid on your performance improvement journey. Below, they are briefly summarized to refer you back to the chapters in which these topics had been dealt with in more detail.

Here's how to use the summary below. Rate your organization on each of these main success factors. A score of one (1) means that your organization exhibits that characteristic to a very limited degree; a score of five (5) demonstrates a high commitment to this principle. Once you have completed the checklist, begin with your weakest points (the issues that received the lowest scores) and review the applicable chapters.

	Score/ Rating	Chapter Reference
1. **Management Commitment** Management drives the initiative and visibly reinforces its importance throughout the entire organization.	1 2 3 4 5	1
2. **Business Case** *Attention to Issues* Focus is on the right issues, and there is clear attention on the right sub-strategies and action required to support this.	1 2 3 4 5	1, 2, 3, 6
Focus on Revenue and Costs The business case portrays a good balance between costs, improvements, revenue enhancements and benefits to be achieved.	1 2 3 4 5	1, 3, 9
Resourcing Adequate resources are dedicated to the initiative. These resources include people and their time, financial resources and technology.	1 2 3 4 5	2, 5, 8
3. **Performance Standards** Performance is continuously compared against baseline measures or established standards.	1 2 3 4 5	3, 4, 5, 10

	Score/ Rating	Chapter Reference

4. CRM Culture

Communication   1 2 3 4 5   7, 10
Communication is a continuous
activity throughout the initiative.
It maintains awareness and supports
the process of continuous improvement.

Resistance to Change   1 2 3 4 5   10
Culture change is being accomplished
easily/effectively.

5. Transition Planning

Prioritization   1 2 3 4 5   1, 2, 9
Consideration is being given to splitting
the initiative into a number of individual
projects, with pilots in some cases.

Structure and Teams   1 2 3 4 5   5, 8
Cross-functional teams or councils
are formed as part of the performance
improvement initiative.

Training and Education   1 2 3 4 5   5, 8, 10
People have the tools and training to
implement required improvement
opportunities successfully. They
understand their roles and have the
skills and knowledge to fill these roles.

SUMMARY

As we move into the twenty-first century, success will be more difficult to achieve. Organizations that will be most successful will be fast, flexible and obsessed with continuous improvement. And that has been the premise of this book.

Performance driven CRM is an ongoing mechanism, based on continuous improvement. It starts with a clear understanding of:

a) the customers, and their needs

b) the organization, and its competencies

c) the organization's commitment to quality service, from both an internal and external customer perspective

It requires measures/standards and benchmarks against each of these, based on fact, not passion, and a desired end state. Lastly, it requires a mechanism to create change—change in process, actions, technology, organizational structure and people competencies. CRM can survive only with continuous performance improvement. And that is what this book has been about—the mechanism/route map on how to achieve lasting performance driven CRM.

You have your guidebook in hand. Good luck on your journey! And, as the old Chinese proverb suggests "the longest journey begins with a single step." May you reach your destination.

Glossary

After Call Work
Time taken to complete a customer transaction after the call has terminated, usually expressed in seconds.

Agent or Customer Service Representative (CSR)
A general term for someone who handles telephone calls in a customer contact center. Other common names for the same job include, but are not limited to, operator, attendant, representative, customer support representative, telephone sales representative, technical support representative (TSR), inside salesperson, telephone salesperson and telemarketer.

Automated Call Distributor (ACD)
An ACD is telephone equipment that directs calls to agents who are most appropriate to service the caller's needs. It ensures that the first call to arrive is the first call answered, and provides the means to specify the many possible variations in the order of calls and agents. An ACD also provides detailed reports on every aspect of the call transaction, including how many calls were connected to the system, how many calls reached the agent, how long the longest call waited for the agent and the average length of each call.

Customer Contact Center
Generally, the definition reflects a facility where customer interactions
are answered or initiated in high volume for the purpose of sales, marketing, customer service, telemarketing, technical support or other specialized business activity. On occasion, the terms "call center" and
"contact center" are used interchangeably. IDC defines the call center
and the customer contact center as follows:

- **Call Center:** A call center is defined as a dedicated facility equipped
  with specialized communication equipment capable of handling
  large volumes of both inbound and outbound telephone calls. Call
  centers handle various types of customer interaction activities such
  as sales, financial transactions, order entry, billing inquiries, account
  maintenance, support, service dispatch, scheduling, general information, technical support etc. Some key technologies in call centers
  include private branch exchanges (PBXs), automated call distributors (ACDs), interactive voice response (IVRs) systems (IVRs), computer telephony integration (CTI) software, call management
  software, customer interaction applications, voice recognition and
  natural language and knowledge bases.

- **Customer contact center:** The traditional call center is currently
  evolving into what should more accurately be called a "customer
  contact center." Technological development (the Internet being a
  primary factor) and changing market needs are essentially transitioning call centers from a corporate operational cost center into a
  strategically significant business process. The focus is changing
  from "handling" customer calls to "maximizing customer value"
  through "meaningful interaction."

Call Vector (VDN)
A series of commands or call processing steps that determine how calls
are handled or routed. Call vectoring offers more flexibility in managing
incoming call traffic, assuring that the best qualified agent answers calls
quickly.

Computer Telephony Integration (CTI)
A term for connecting computer workstations and file servers through
a local area network to a telephone switch and allowing the computer
to issue the switch commands to route calls. The classic application for
CTI is in call centers.

Computer Contact Software

The desktop application that provides sales and service software to handle fulfillment as well as case management and contact history functionality.

Customer Care Center

A term created by Alex Szlam, the president of Melita International, to describe a telephone call center with three basic elements: "...the database technology and marketing savvy to fill that database with individual customer preference information; the ability to handle inbound calls; and the ability to make outbound calls."

Digital Recorder

A device that digitally records conversations with callers. Digital recorders allow the conversion of aural (sound) information into a series of pulses that are translated into a binary code intelligible to computer circuits. The information recorded in this way can be stored in many ways, including as information in a computer. Other recorders are cassette-style with standard speed and slow extended play speed, while some are reel-to-reel and have the same features as the cassettes.

Ergonomics

The science of determining proper relationships between mechanical and computerized devices and personal comfort and convenience— how a telephone handset should be shaped, how a keyboard should be laid out. Ergonomics are of particular importance for customer contact center employees.

Field Service/Support

Field service/support refers to the enabling of customer care processes to support field service and support functions. This definition centers on the reengineering of a company's customer care systems and processes to enable field employees to access corporate systems while in the field. This definition does not focus on the devices or applications used by these field employees but on how companies support and integrate these field functions into their customer care systems and processes.

Gate

Also known as a split, group or skill. These elements usually refer to a set of agents served by an ACD. In the ACD's routing scheme, the gate, group or skill is a set of agents that are all qualified to handle the same type of call. A customer contact center could operate with a single gate, group or skill, meaning any call could go to any agent. In larger centers multiple gates, groups or skills are common.

Host
This term usually refers to a common central computer. In an all-computer setup, it is the computer that contains common applications used by multiple workstations.

Knowledge Base
A help desk or technical support term. It is a collection of information about a particular subject, usually in question and answer format, or a series of if-then statements. The system uses artificial intelligence to mimic human problem solving. It applies the rules stored in the knowledge base engine and the data supplies to the system to solve a particular business problem or to answer a specific question.

Marketing Automation
Marketing automation (MA) primarily involves front-office software applications used to automate corporate marketing efforts such as the organization and collection of customer data, the management and analysis of campaigns, database marketing and marketing personalization. An emerging segment of CRM, MA software coordinates a company's overall marketing strategy and activities as implemented through the contact center, e-business, direct mailings or trade shows.

Middleware
Software that transmits transactions between customer contact centers and back-end systems. For example, an order placed through the e-store is transmitted to both the customer contact center and order fulfillment application.

Reader Board
A large sign displayed in the customer contact center, which displays up-to-the-minute ACD and CSR statistics. The display is usually made up of LEDs. The statistics are updated frequently, usually every 30 seconds. Common statistics displayed are the number of calls in queue, the amount of time that the longest call has been holding and the average speed of answer and service level.

Real-Time Adherence
Usually a "near-real time" visual display of current agent activity being compared to scheduled agent activity.

Sales Automation Software

Sometimes referred to as sales force automation (SFA), it is a program that allows for rapid and orderly maintenance of contact records by salespeople either at the office or in the field. It should allow them to send follow-up literature, schedule calls and letters and access a customer's history. There are many configurations of sales automation software, ranging from a simple record-keeping program on a PC to a complex, multiuser database that connects LANs and laptops. Sales automation software includes products specifically designed to meet the routine and strategic needs of the sales organization and its representatives. Sales automation products help the sales professional organize and collect information about territories, customers, products, competitors, marketing campaigns, and pricing. Features include, at a minimum, some combination of a customer database, lead qualification, an integrated word processor, a report writer, an address and phone card system and a tickler file. In addition, many products now offer an opportunity management system, sales order or sales configuration tools, a marketing encyclopedia, reporting and forecasting functionality and some kind of Internet or Web access—allowing rapid and global information sharing within a company and between companies.

Service Bureau

A company that provides customer contact center services for other companies. Some of the services that can be done are inbound and outbound calling, managing a list of names and numbers, fulfillment, demographic analysis, direct mail, fundraising and disaster planning.

Service Level

The customer contact center's customer service measurement. This measure may be determined by analyzing the number of seconds callers wait before a CSR answers their calls. The measurement of service level is usually expressed as a percentage of calls answered within a target number of seconds compared to the total number of calls.

Speech Recognition

A technology that enables a machine to understand a human voice. It allows input into a computer or telephone system through spoken words. A common example is a cellular telephone that can be dialed by speaking the number of digits to be dialed. In customer contact centers, speech recognition is often used to replace the touch tone keypad in IVR applications.

Systems Integration

The process of integrating various technologies and applications to operate as a cohesive system to provide competitive business advantage.

Technology Integration

Historically, there are many disparate systems within customer contact centers: ACD, IVR, order management, customer tracking, knowledge base, A/R, shipping, inventory, contracts etc. Technology integration promotes an environment that is technically seamless from system to system. Enterprise customer contact centers must deploy seamless systems in order to capture and identify their customers' market needs.

Touch Points

Your customer experiences your company at a touch point. A touch point is the intersection of a business event (such as a product inquiry, order taking, customer referral or campaign response) taking place via a channel (telephone, Web, mobile, direct sales, third party, retail) using a media (face to face, mail, telephone, fax, kiosk or IVR). Your ability to add value at each touch point determines the quality of your customer's experience. Noncustomer touch points are typically technology components that enable the effective and efficient operation of customer touch points. For example, data warehousing and data mining are tools used for both CRM and non-CRM applications; when applied to a CRM solution such as marketing automation, they can significantly improve an enterprise's intelligence regarding its customers and have an impact on how that enterprise interacts with its customers.

Virtual Customer Contact Center

A virtual customer contact center consists of several groups of agents, usually in separate locations, that are treated as a single center for call handling purposes.

Voice Recognition

An application that allows entry into the system by authenticating the voice of the customer accessing the system.

Wireless Application Protocol (WAP)

Devices that use the Internet to transmit and process data through a wireless device such as a pager or phone.

Web-Based CRM

Web-based CRM encompasses the same customer touch point activities previously conducted through more established channels. Web-based CRM services are distinct from Internet services that design, build and maintain corporate Web sites and other e-commerce systems and initiatives.

Web Collaboration

A Java-based, enterprise-class application that allows customer contact center agents, sales and service representatives to visually interact with customers or prospects over the Web during any telephone call. To participate in a Web session, remote callers require only a Java-enabled browser—no special software downloads are necessary. Once connected via Web session, representatives can share static and dynamic Web content, demonstrate software, navigate callers around the Web and instantly transfer downloadable files.

Workstation

The computer industry tends to refer to workstations as high-speed personal computers, which are used for high-powered processing tasks such as CAD/CAM or engineering.

Building Your Performance Improvement Plan (PIP)

Now that you have determined your current performance and know to what extent you want to improve, it is time to build your performance improvement plan (PIP). You know what you want to accomplish and now is the time to commit to improving and mapping out your route to success.

A performance improvement plan can be compared to a road map.

There are four steps to building your plan.

Step 1: Deciding What to Include

Step 2: Completing your "Performance Improvement" template

Step 3: Creating your "Performance Improvement Oath"

Step 4: Committing to your first three improvement areas

STEP 1: Deciding What to Include

The following checklist should be completed for EVERY performance area you want to improve. This checklist will guide you to completing your PIP. Where appropriate, if all of your answers are positive, you can include the performance area in your PIP. If not, you may want to revisit the significance the performance area has to your overall improvement goal.

The performance area I want to focus on is:
Is it necessary for me to focus on this area? Why? (Justify your answer to yourself. Weight the efforts against the outcomes and rewards.)
Will I achieve benefits by focusing on this area for "me"?
Will I achieve benefits by focusing on this area for "my employer"?
Will I achieve benefits by focusing on this area for "my family and friends"?
Do I know how to improve in this area?
Do I lack the knowledge and skills to improve in this area? Do I not know how to do it?
What information do I already have to help me improve?
What information do I still need to improve?
How can I make improving in this area any simpler?
How long have I needed improvement in this area?

STEP 2: Completing Your Performance Improvement Template

What is my priority?	How will I measure myself?	What will my target be?	How will I identify and celebrate success?
1.			
2.			
3.			
4.			
5.			
6.			
7.			
8.			
9.			
10.			

STEP 3: Creating Your Performance Improvement Oath

I commit to ...	I commit to doing this	I am unable to commit to doing this	I am able/unable to commit to doing this because...
Improving my performance.	❏	❏	❏
Being patient —it takes time. Sometimes improvement is one small step at a time. Don't rush it.	❏	❏	❏
Being persistent —Stick with it.	❏	❏	❏
Being realistic— Don't try to improve too much at once in too short of a time.	❏	❏	❏
Being focused— This requires planning and discipline.	❏	❏	❏
Completing another self-test in six months and comparing the scores.	❏	❏	❏
Rewarding myself if I have improved.	❏	❏	❏

STEP 4: Committing to Your First Three Areas: I Will Improve In...

Now that you have identified the areas in which you want to improve, it is a good idea to know how much improvement you need and what steps you are going to take. Setting a performance improvement date will also help you achieve your PIP—one step at a time.

Insert the performance improvement that you want to focus on over the next six weeks in the area below, and rate how much improvement is needed. You must do this for three different areas. Then determine three action steps you will take to improve this performance area and your due date.

Performance Improvement Area:

Area ————————————————————————

1   2   3   4   5

(little)   (lots)

Action Steps

1. _____

2. _____

3. _____

My Due Date

D D / M M / Y Y
_____

How Will I Know If I Am Successful?

You have achieved success if you have become:

❑ Fast-paced

❑ Responsible and accountable

❑ Pleasurable to be with

❑ Humorous

❑ Quick to adapt

❑ Self-sufficient (don't need as much direction)

❑ Motivated

❑ Focused on quality

❑ Supportive of others

❑ Professional

But Don't Give Into....

- Impatience
- Not listening
- Being passive
- Being inappropriate
- Leaving others behind
- Going off in the wrong direction
- Being thin-skinned

Excellence is doing ordinary things
extraordinarily well.

—John W. Gardner

Index